Calais

...g ...s, Middlesex HA8 8XE

| | |
|---|---|
| Written By: | Sharron Livingston |
| Published By: | Passport Guide Publications |
| Enquiries : | Tel: 020 8905 4851 |
| Email: | Sharron@channelhoppers.net |
| Web site: | www.channelhoppers.net |
| | |
| Advertising | Logie Bradshaw Media Ltd |
| Enquiries: | Tel:  01442 233331 |
| | Fax: 01442 231131 |

The Channel Hoppers Series

ISBN: 1-903390-00-1

# Contents

# Contents

## Shopping and leisure
## What a pleasure!

While there are high levels of duty levied on Britain's wine lovers, the lure of the vinous bargains across the Channel are simply irresistible. Millions of daytrippers, weekenders and those in need of a short break choose northern France to fulfill their shopping and leisure hopes. But for most cross-Channel bargain buying hopefuls, some important questions need answers:

What are the bargains? Where do you buy them? Where do you eat, sleep and sightsee?

The Channel Hopper's Guide has the answers. The following pages are packed with interesting wine recommendations along with many other shopping ideas.

We at the Channel Hopper's Guide have done all the legwork for you and tasted more than 400 wines, so you'll know exactly where to go and what is worthwhile to buy.

And if you're staying for a night or two, we have made hotel and restaurant suggestions including help with the French menu.

But best of all are the many special offers negotiated for you, our readers, to add extra value to your trip.

So don't forget to take the Channel Hopper's Guide with you before you set off. Just slip it into your passport wallet. You'll find it's conveniently exactly the same size.

*Bon Voyage....*

## Meet the team at this year's
## Channel Hoppers Guide Wine Tasting

**Robert Joseph**
Robert is publishing editor of Wine Magazine and Wine & Spirits International. He has authored over 20 books on wine and is the editor of the Sunday Telegraph Good Wine Guide. He is chairman and co-chairman of the International Wine Challenge in London and Asia. His expertise as a wine consultant is sought around the world.

**Anthony Rose**
Anthony is wine correspondent of The Independent, a regular contributor to Wine Magazine, Decanter, Harpers, Winepros.com and has co-authored the annual wine guide, Grapevine. He teaches wine at Leith's School of Food & Wine and judges wine competitions around the globe. Last year he won the Glenfiddich & Lanson Black Label Wine Writer of the Year awards.

**Richard Bampfield MW**
Having spent most of his working life managing wine businesses on his way to becoming a Master of Wine, Richard is now an established wine consultant, educator and judge. He isalso an experienced 'Bon Vivant' whose expertise at wine events is greatly sought. **www.winevents.co.uk**
**Tel: 01628 638131**

**Sharron Livingston**
Sharron, an established travel writer, is frequently featured in the national media. She has authored a series of Channel Hoppers Guides. As a wine enthusiast, she was dismayed at the amount of unpalatable wine millions of Britons were buying across the Channel due to the lack of meaningful information. In reponse she created the annual Channel Hopper's Guide Wine Tasting in order to fill this void.

# Hopping Over

Cross-Channel hopping has become a familiar aspect of British life and with the levels of duty on alcohol and tobacco still so high and the pound so strong, Le Shopping Trip and Le Weekend Away are still as enticing as ever.

The cost of cross-Channel travel fluctuates with the seasons and the promotions offered by different operators. It is best to shop around for a good deal.

Alternatively, you could delegate the whole process to a travel club, especially if you are looking to combine your shopping trip with a mini break.

> If you are looking to stay overnight in Dover contact the Dover Guest House Association
> Tel: 01304 210397
> or visit their web-site:
> www.doveraccommodation.co.uk

## Hopping Over

# Hopping Over

The perks of shopping abroad start on board where products are available at low French duty paid prices.

| Crossing | From/To | Journey Time | Frequency |
|---|---|---|---|
| **Hoverspeed:** Seacat Tel: 08705 240 241 www.hoverspeed.co.uk Bus toRailway Station. Fare: £1 | Dover/ Calais Check-in: 20 mins | 40 mins | Up to 10 sailings daily |
| **Eurotunnel** Tel: 0990 353535 www.eurotunnel.com No foot passengers. Vehicles only. | Folkestone/ Calais Turn up Check-in: 20 mins | 35 mins | Every 15 mins peak time |
| **P&O Stena Line** Tel: 0990 980980 www.posl.com Free bus service to Calais town centre | Dover/Calais Check-in: 30 mins | 75 mins | Every 45 mins peak time |
| **SeaFrance:** Tel: 0990 711711 www.seafrance.com Free bus service to Calais town centre | Dover/ Calais Check-in: 45 mins | 90 mins | Every 90 mins peak time |
| **Norfolkline:** Tel: 0870 870 1020 doverpax@norfolkline.com www.norfolkline.com | Dover/ Dunkerque Check-in: 60 mins | 120 mins | 6 times a day peak time |

# FANTASTIC VIEWS.
## INE WINES. SUPERB FOOD.

# ND THAT'S BEFORE YOU
# EVEN ARRIVE IN FRANCE.

# How Do You Say?

**Pleasantries**

| | |
|---|---|
| Nice to meet you | Enchanté |
| Yes/No | Oui/non |
| Good Morning/Good Day | Bonjour |
| How are you? | Ça va |
| Good Evening/Good Night/Good Bye | Bonsoir/Bonne nuit/Au revoir |
| Excuse me | Excusez-moi |
| Thank you | Merci |
| You're welcome | Je vous en prie |

**Being Understood**

| | |
|---|---|
| I don't speak French | Je ne parle pas français |
| I don't understand | Je ne comprends pas |
| Do you speak English? | Parlez-vous anglais? |
| I don't know how to say it in French | Je ne sais pas le dire en français |

**Eating Out**

| | |
|---|---|
| A table for two please | Une table pour deux, s'il vous plaît |
| The menu please | Le menu, s'il vous plaît |
| Do you have a children's menu? | Avez-vous un menu pour les enfants? |
| We'll take the set menu please | Nous prendrons le menu, s'il vous plaît |
| We would like a dessert | Nous aimerions du dessert |
| The bill please | L'addition, s'il vous plaît |
| Is service included? | Le service est compris? |
| Do you accept credit cards? | Acceptez-vous les cartes de crédit? |

**Hotels**

| | |
|---|---|
| I'd like a single/double room | Je voudrais une chambre pour une personne/deux personnes |
| I reserved a room in the name of | J'ai réservé une chambre au nom de |
| I confirmed my booking by phone/letter | J'ai confirmé ma réservation par téléphone/lettre |
| My key please | Ma clé, s'il vous plaît |
| I shall be leaving tomorrow | Je partirai demain |
| What time is breakfast/dinner | Le petit déjeuner/Le dîner est à quelle heure? |

**Paying**

| | |
|---|---|
| How much is it? | Ça coûte combien? |
| I'd like to pay please | On veut payer, s'il vous plaît |
| Can I have the bill please? | L'addition, s'il vous plaît |
| Can I pay by credit card? | Puis-je payer avec une carte de credit? |
| Do you accept traveller's cheques/Eurocheques/sterling? | Acceptez-vous les cheques de voyages/Eurocheques/sterling? |

# AA Five Star Europe

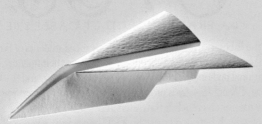

# You remember French Classes, don't you?

*But do you remember enough to deal with a breakdown abroad on you own?*

*worry? AA Five Star European Breakdown Assistance nnects you with our English-speaking incident team, who will provide the help and support you need 24 hours a day.*

Call today on **0800 0857 241** (ref. PCH1)

*Don't let breaking down be the most*

# Dunkerque

*It's Dunkirk in English, Dunkerque in French but both words are derived from the Flemish term - Dune Kerk - The Church of the Dunes*

During the first millenium Dunkerque gradually developed from an inhospitable mass of silt washed over by raging seas from the Flemish coast into a thriving hamlet of fisherman. By natural design a series of dunes had formed consequently keeping the sea at bay and creating the lowlands.

The fishing community were of religious Christian persuasion and thus they built a church on the top of one of the dunes. In recognition of this, the town was named 'The Church of the Dunes' - Dunkirk/Dunkerque.

Being just a fishing port, Dunkerque was easily vanquished by the Spanish, French, English and Dutch. During the Battle of the Dunes in 1658 the Flemish Protestants gave Dunkerque over to Oliver Cromwell in exchange for the help of his Ironside troops in fighting off the Spanish. In 1662 Charles II sold Dunkerque back to the French for 5,000,000 livres, to be ruled by "Sun King" Louis XIV.

World War II brought mass destruction to Dunkerque. On 10th May, overwhelmed by the menacing German advance, Allied troops were driven back onto the beach at Dunkerque. The huge numbers of Allied troops were trapped and as they had nowhere else to go but into the sea they had become an easy target. So it was into the sea they went. "Operation Dynamo" called upon every available ship or boat to help evacuate 335,000 allied troops.

After five years of German bombardment, Dunkerque was almost entirely demolished. Both the town and its economy had to be rebuilt. Through a process of rapid commercial and industrial expansion, Dunkerque today is regarded as France's third largest port.

Though Dunkerque has remained in French hands ever since1662 the gastronomy available in restaurants, the festivals and flamboyant, colourfull street carnivals betray an innate Flemish culture and cuisine.

---

**How to get to Dunkerque Town Centre**
Dunkerque town centre is a full fifteen-minute drive from the ferry.

Take the A16 motorway in the direction of Ostend and exit at juncton 33 following signs to Dunkerque Centre. Turn left onto Avenue Rosendal which quickly turns into Boulevard St Barbe and follow signs to Centre Ville.

**The Tourist Office**
Le Belfroi
rue de l'Amiral Ronarc'h
59140 Dunkerque
Tel: 00 33 (0)3 28 66 79 21
Open: Mon-Sat
Closes 12.30-1.30 Mon-Fri

Following on from the above directions:
Turn right after the Jean Bart Square. You will see the belfry in front of the church. The tourist office is located inside the belfry.

# Dunkerque

### *Who Is Jean Bart?*

The townsfolk of Dunkerque are proud to present the most celebrated corsair in French history - Jean Bart. A local hero whose memory transcends time by remaining firmly entrenched in the hearts of the people for more than three centuries, for he is the man who saved France from famine. His legacy is clearly felt everywhere in the town.

He certainly had all the qualities of a hero. He started life as the son of an ordinary fishing and privateering family. His brilliant career saw him rise through the ranks to the nobility but he always maintained his straight talking and simple demeanour.

His heroic path started when as a young man he joined the naval service under the Dutch Admiral Michiel de Ruyter. Nevertheless his allegiance always remained with France and when war broke out between the French and the Dutch (1672-78) he returned to Dunkerque to command a French fleet of small privateering vessels. In just six battles he captured 81 ships. Louis XIV rewarded him by promoting him to the rank of Lieutenant Commander of the Royal Navy.

When he was wounded and taken prisoner by the English during the War of the Grand Alliance (1689-97) he promptly escaped. He rowed from Plymouth for a marathon 52 days until he reached the

# Dunkerque

French coast. He made the English pay dearly for his treatment by capturing innumerable English ships.

His finest hour came when in 1696 his country faced famine. He set out with a Dutch squadron and captured 130 ships laden with Russian and Polish wheat, thereby saving the people of France from inevitable starvation.

His heroism was rewarded in 1694 when he was elevated to the ranks o the nobility with a peerage.

Just another three years later the Sun King Louis XIV personally announced a further appointment by saying: "Jean Bart, I have appointed you to the rank of Commodore." Without mincing his words, Jean Bart promptly replied: "Sire, you were right to do so."

Jean Bart statue by David Angers (1848) located on Place Jean-Bart

## Musée Portuaire

9 quai de la Citadelle
59140 Dunkerque
Tel: 00 33 (0)328 63 33 39
Within this former 19th-century tobacco warehouse is a museum of the history of Dunkerque port. The workings of the port are explained in detail with the help of maps, paintings, engravings, dioramas, model ships and samples of tools used by dockers. As Dunkerque was once the main privateering harbour, with Jean Bart at the helm, there are of course many illustrations of his exploits There are two different portraits of the corsair, though no one actually knows what he looked like. Situated in front of the museum are some old ships.
Open daily (except Tues) 10.00 to 12.45 and 13.30 to 18.00
Entry fee applies.

## Belfroi

Rue de L'Amiral Ronarc'h
59140 Dunkerque
Tel: 00 33 (0)328 66 79 21
The Belfry doubles as the tourist office, and is anhistorical monument. it was once attached to the Church of St-Etoi but the church burnt down in 1558. It towers some 58m/190ft over the town and ifyou climb the 60 steps, you will get a good view of the town and see the 48 bells which play "Jean Bart's tune" on the hour,and other popular tunes every 15 mintues.

## Hotel de Ville

Place Charles Valentin
59140 Dunkerque
Tel: 00 33 (0)328 26 26 26
The stylish town hall, built by Louis Cordonnier has Félix Gaudin's stained glass window highlighting Jean Bart's victorious return from war.

# Dunkerque Sights

**Musée des Beaux-Arts**
Place du Général de Gaulle
59140 Dunkerque
Tel: 00 33 (0)328 59 21 65
The Fine Arts museum is rich with paintings dating from the 16th to the 20th century..There is an impressive panel of 540 Delft tiles located in the entrance hall which protray the bombardment of Dunkerque in 1695. Naturally, the local hero Jean Bart has most of the ground floor filled with historical items concerning his exploits. Other floors cover the Flemish, dutch and French schools of arts. Open daily from 10.00 to 12.15 and 1.45 to 18.00 except Tues. Tariff: 20F

**Le Phare**
Route des Ecluse
59140 Dunkerque
Tel: 00 33 (0)28 63 33 99
Anyone can visit the lighthouse between June and September.

---

### Outdoor Leisure

**Dunkerque Golf Club**
Route du Golf
Coudekerque Village
18-hole golf course with many water obstacles.
Tel: 00 33 (0)328 61 07 43
Take the A16 motorway and exit junction 31 in the direction of Coudekerque and Bergue

---

#### Special Offer

Show your guide and get 15% discount on the cost of your game.

---

**Boat Trips**
Boat trips can be arranged at the tourist office. There are three trips lasting between 60-105 minutes.
* The commercial port
* The industrial adventure
* The industrial adventure by night
Tariffs from £3.50
Daily in July and August, otherwise weekends only.

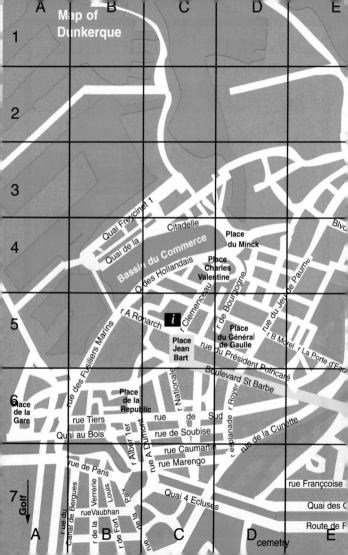

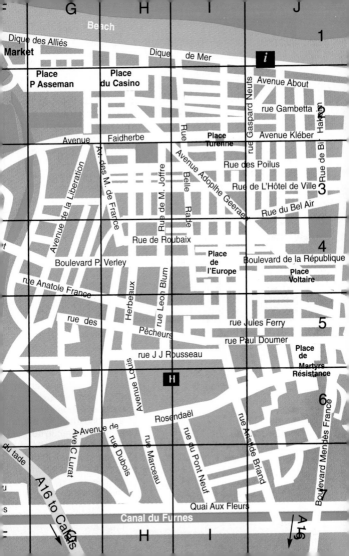

## Auchan Hypermarket

**Auchan Hypermarket**
Route National 40
59760 Grande Synthe
Dunkerque
00 33 (0)3 28  58 55 55
www.auchan.fr

Map Ref:    Follow G7
Bus No:
English:    A little
Tasting:    No
Payment:    £, 💳 💳
Parking:    Yes
Open:       8.30 to 20.30
Closed:     Sunday

**How to Get There**
From the port continue straight on for 800 metres and take fourth exit at the roundabout (N1) direction Dunkerque-Port Est. 4km later it is on the right hand side Centre Commercial.
or
Take A16 motorway, exit 25 signposted Centre Commercial, Grande Synthe.

Dunkerque has two hypermarkets, Auchan, the largest and Carrefour. Best buys are not only the wines (which are exclusively French) beers and champagnes, but also mustard, olives, bicycles, garden furniture and baby car seats and accessories.

## Carrefour Hypermarket

**Carrefour Hypermarket**
Saint Pol
59430 Saint Pol sur Mer
00 33 (0)3 28  58 58 58
www.carrefour.fr

Map Ref:
Bus No:
English:    A little
Tasting:    No
Payment::   💳 💳
Parking:    Yes
Open:       8.30-19.30
Closed:     Sunday

**How to Get There**
From the port take A16 motorway. Exit at junction 29 and second exit off the roundabout, cross over the traffic lights, and next roundabout, then turn left at the second traffic lights turn left entering avenue de Petite Synthe (sign St Pol Sur Mer - Centre). At the second traffic lights turn right over a bridge towards Centre Commercial.

# Cave Paul Herpe Wine Merchant

Cave Paul Herpe
208 rue de la République
Saint Pol Sur Mer
00 33 (0)3 28 60 99 19

Map Ref: J4
Bus No: -
English: A little
Tasting: En Vrac wines
Payment: £, 💳 💳
Parking: Yes
Open: 09.00-19.30
Sun 09.00-12.30
Closed: 12.30-14.30
All day Monday

**How to Get There**
From the port take A16 motorway. Exit at junction 29 and firstt exit of the roundabout following sign to St Pol Sur Mer-Carnot. At the next roundabout take second exit (ie. straight across), left at the junction and continue straight over the traffic lights following signs to St Pol Sur Mer. At the next set of lights turn left following signs to Centre Ville into Rue de la République and continue for five minutes.

Cave Paul Herpe belongs to a chain of shops which specialise in the wines of the Languedoc region.

At Cave Paul Herpe you have the choice of buying your wine the French way en vrac (draught), or in bottles.  For a small charge you buy a 10L or 20L container called a cubi and fill it with any one of the wines available en vrac.  These start at a simple table wine for 93p per litre to a sweet Muscat de Riversaltes AOC,  the wine the Languedoc is most famous for - at £4.20 a litre.

# Le Chais Transat

Le Chais Transat
25 rue du Gouvernement
Dunkerque
00 33 (0) 328 63 78 52
www.caves-transat.fr

Map Ref:   C4
English:   A little
Tasting:   No
Payment:   💳 💳
Parking:   Yes
Open:      09.00-19.00
Closed:    Sun and Mon

Le Chais Transat was once part of the famous Compagnie Générale Transatlantique known simply as Transat. For 120 years the company ran a fleet of luxury liners. When the last made her final voyage in 1974, a depot was opened in Le Havre to sell off the stock. Transat had always symbolised high quality to the public who rushed to buy what they could. To satisfy this demand a trading company was set-up later developing into a chain of outlets. Inside this branch, you will be met with an orderly layout of quality French wines and champagnes displayed on their boxes. There are some vin de table starting at 13F but most wines are in the 50F-100F bracket. Service is not rushed so you may as well take your time.

**How to Get There**

Take the A16 motorway in the direciton of Ostend and exit at juncton 33 following signs to Dunkerque Centre. Turn left onto Avenue Rosendal which quickly turns into Boulevard St Barbe to Centre Ville. Turninto Jean Bart Square, continue to Place Charles Valentin and Place du Minck. After you enter the citadelle the shop is situated behind the port museum.

**SPECIAL OFFER:**
Show your guide and receive a
**5%**
discount on purchases

# Le Blockhaus d'Eperlecques

-10 FF

A t the fringe of the forest of Eperlecques, you will find a gigantic bunker. "Blockhous" constructed during the Second World War, it has been preserved since 1945 as it was, At that time, a launching site for the V1.

It's here that the last existing, launching ramp in Europe, for the V1, some 150 feet in length, is exposed.

The visit to this woodland park with its historic and authentic monument is well commentated, and you can compare, the 2 german arms of reprisal, the V1 and V2. Today the "Blockhouse of Eperlecques" is open as a monument to peace.

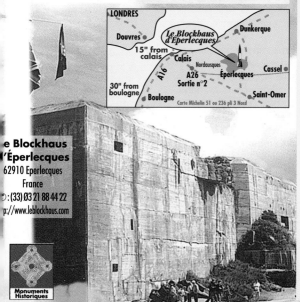

LONDRES

Le Blockhaus d'Eperlecques

Douvres

Dunkerque

15" from calais

Calais

Nordausques

Cassel

A26 Sortie n°2

Éperlecques

30" from boulogne

Boulogne

Saint-Omer

Carte Michelin 51 ou 236 pli 3 Nord

Le Blockhaus d'Éperlecques
62910 Eperlecques
France
☎ : (33) 03 21 88 44 22
http://www.leblockhaus.com

Monuments Historiques

**On presentation of this reduction coupon a 10 FF reduction is offered on the entrance fee to the Blockhouse.**

# Calais Town

**Calais is the closest French port to England and the evident touristic appeal centres around shopping. But is that all Calais has to offer?**

**H**aving suffered the ravages of war, Calais was completely rebuilt after World War II. Most people now see this port as a lattice-work of commercial streets, conveniently located solely to enjoy the benefits of cheaper shopping. Right?

Well, maybe not. Its well established cross-Channel links and its geographical location makes it a good starting point to many destinations. The motorway network via the A26 and A16 means easy journeys to Belgium, Strasbourg, Paris, Germany and of course the rest of France.

But those staying a while will see that Calais is really three towns in one: Calais-Nord, Calais-Sud and Calais-Ouest. Calais-Nord is the harbour area and is home to rue Royale, considered to be the smartest shopping street. It also has the smartest restaurants. Calais-Sud is the main town centre with a variety of shops and department stores. Calais-Ouest is where Cité Europe shopping complex

## How to Get From the Port to the Town Centre

Follow the **Toutes Directions** sign. At the roundabout take the fourth exit signposted **Centre Ville**. Turn left at the next roundabout, drive along the canal and at the traffic lights turn right. This leads to the square in front of the Town Hall with Calais-Nord to your right and Calais-Sud to the left. Turning right leads you to the seafront, rue Royale and Place d'Armes.

is located. Its ultra-modern building contrasts sharply with the nearby ruined fortifications.

Aside from its commercial aspect, the Calais area has a good range of leisure activities. The vast sandy beaches are popular with both the locals and tourists. There are numerous acitivities on offer such as sailing, sail boarding, speed sailing, sand yachting, water skiing or just plain sun bathing.

It generally comes as a surprise to first-time visitors, but the surrounding area's beautiful countryside is ideal for a leisurely stroll, off-road cycling, horse riding and even fishing.

And if all of this is too much, you can always take one of the canal cruises along the waterways that criss-cross the Marais Audomarois and contemplate your next shopping trip!

### Cycle Hire
**VTT Brame Sports**
178 Boulevard la Fayette
Calais

### Canal Cruises
**Marais Audomarois**
Nature Park Audomarois
Tel:00 33 (0) 321 98 62 98

**La Grange Nature de Claimarais**
Tel: 00 33 (0)321 95 23 40
Fishing,, rowing boats, boat trips and canan ('watergang') cruises.

### Offshore Cruises
For information about sailing down the Côte d'Opale on the yacht Ophelie to Cap Blanc-Nez
Tel: 00 33 (0)231 93 63 71
or contact the tourist office.

### Riding
**Cheval Loisir**
182 route de Gravelines
Calais
Tel: 00 33 (0)321 971 818
Escorted countryside rides.

### Water Ski
**Le Club de la Gravière**
Blerio-Plage
Tel: 00 33 (0) 321 34 63 50

# Calais Sights

**T**ake in a few sights while in Calais. After all it was under English rule for more than 200 years during the occupation of 1347-1558.

### Hôtel de Ville, place du Soldat Inconnu

One of Calais' finest landmarks is the Town Hall which can be seen for miles around. This magnificent Flemish-style structure built of brick and stone, was completed in 1925 and dominates the main square. It houses many paintings and is adorned with stained-glass windows which tells the story of the departing English. It also acts to diffuse the sunlight around the grand staircase. The interior is renowned for the elaborate decor of the reception rooms. Also attached to the town hall is an ornate brick clock tower and belfry which stands 74m/246ft high. The chimes of its bells are most appealing. Visiting hours 08.00-12.00 and 13.30-17.30

### Rodin's Six Burghers place du Soldat Inconnu

At the foot of the clock tower and Town Hall stands Rodin's original 19th-century bronze statue of the Burghers of Calais. The bronze work, consist of six statues recalling the final year of the Hundred Years War. The mayor, with other prominent citizens assembled here wearing only their shirts, before surrendering to King Edward II. They were willing to sacrifice their lives to save Calais from being massacred by Edward at the end of his

Les Six Bourgeois de Calais

The Town Hall. Inset : Rodin's Burghers

six-month siege. Their heroism moved the King's French wife, Philippine of Hainault, to plead successfully for their pardon.

Take a moment to examine each statue. Notice the veins and the clenched muscles, and the tension in their torsos, betraying their proud apprehension about their imminent humiliation.

> **Did You Know..**
> that both Emma Lyons (Nelson's Lady Hamilton) and Beau Brummell sought refuge from creditors in Calais. Lady Hamilton died in Calais at 27 rue Française in 1815 poverty-stricken and thoroughly miserable. A year later Brummell made his way here to avoid his creditors and the displeasure of his former friend the Prince Regent. During his 15-year stay he was known by his first two names George Bryan.

> **Annual Brocante August 16**
> 350 "bric à brac" stalls make this the largest summer street market.

## Parc St. Pierre

The well tended park opposite the town hall offers an idyllic setting for summer picnics . The statue in front of the park is **Monument du Souvenir,** a memorial to the unknown soldier.

## Musée de la Guerre

In the middle of the park is an old camouflaged German bunker. It once a telephone exchange during the World War II, but today serves as a war museum. Inside there are posters, old war-time documents and memorabilia together with historical recollections of the Resistance, Calais' occupation and the Battle of Britain.
The war museum is open daily from 10.00-17.00 from February to December. Entry fee is around £1.50

> **The Tourist Office**
> 21 Bloulevard Clémenceau
> BP 94 62102, Calais
> Tel: 00 33 (0)321 96 62 40
>
> **General Market Days**
> Place de Crève Coeur,
> Place d'Armes
> Wed, Thur, and Sat. am.

### Citadelle
### nr Square Vauban

Dating back to 1560 this was originally built to house the town's garrison after the French retook Calais. Much of the later work is attributable to the French engineer Vauban. Today it is used as a sports centre.

### Place D'Armes

Once upon a time, this was the main bustling area of medieval Calais. Alas, war-time devastation destroyed most of the original square leaving just a 13th- century watchtower as a reminder of this time. This popular square, just a short walk away from the harbour and some fine restaurants, is surrounded by cafés and shops. Three times a week, the car park in the middle turns into a colourful general market.

### Eglise Notre-Dame,
### rue Notre Dame

The architecture of the church is partly English Gothic in style, a legacy of English rule between 1347 and 1558.In 1921 Captain Charles de Gaulle married a local girl call Yvonne Vendroux here.

### Musée de Beaux Arts et
### de la Dentelle
### 25, rue Richelieu

The Museum of Fine Art and Lace houses paintings from the 15th to 20th century and sculpture from19th and 20th centuriy. On display are exhibits of Calais' lace - an industry originating from England. Incidentally the first lace factory was established in Calais at **rue de Vic** in the URSSAF building. The museum is open Wednesday to Monday 10.00-12.00 and 14.00-17.30Entry £1.50.

---

Did You Know.. that the beach at Blériot-Plage (just before the D940 coastal road) is named after the inventor Louis Blériot. He was the first man to cross the channel in a flying machine that was heavier than air. He flew his monoplane from this spot 1909.The annual Blériot Air Show, a tribute to Louis Blériot, is quite an extravaganze of air display and aerobatics. Further information from Sangatte-Blériot-Plage Tourist Office Tel: 00 33 (0)321 34 97 98.

## Calais Insights

### *Rue Royale in Calais Centre has some really good shops. Don't miss them.*

Rodéo Drive at number 40 rue Royale. This small, unpretentious shop, though not a Calvin Klein store, specialises in CK designer wear at around 20% less than the UK prices.

If you like to dine from fine porcelaine, drink from crystal and adorn your home with fine decorative designer items, here is a tip: stylish Lalique and Baccarat crystal, items made by Christophle, porcelain from Royale de Limoges and Versace dinner sets are available at René Classe at 61 Rue Royale. They cost between 20-33% less than normal UK prices!

Anyone for tea? Around 70 varieties can be purchased at Brulerie La Tour at 65 rue Royale. In fact everything you could wish for to enjoy a cuppa is available on their shelves including pretty tea sets, a range of tempting chocolates and and biscuits.

Au Royal Chocolat at number 67 is a quaint chocolate shop. On sale is 'Les Coucougnettes' awarded the 'Best Speciality Sweet in France' by the Salon International de La Confiseries Paris. They were enjoyed by King Henry IV and If you too like marzipan, you will love them. A bag of **Les Coucougnettes** costs £6.90.

Also on Rue Royale is the French version of Toni & Guy hairdressers, Jacques Dessange, inventor of the famous **'Tousled Look'** so loved by women globally. The professional team discuss your hair requirements and because they all have to undergo training at the Jacques Dessange training centre in Paris, you can be sure of a happy result.

# JACQUES DESSANGE

**52 Rue Royale, Calais**
**Tel: 00 33 (0)3 21 96 10 00**

**55 Grande Rue, Boulogne Sur Mer**
**Tel: 00 33 (0)3 21 83 07 14**

**18 Rue Clémenceau, Dunkerque**
**Tel: 00 33 (0)3 28 63 63 06**

## A PASSION TO EXCEL
◆ World Leader in 'Top of the Range' Hairdressing
◆ 660 Hairdressing Salons in 35 countries
◆ Every day, 36,0000 women enter a Jacques Dessange hairdresssing salon

## YOUR BEAUTY WELCOME
◆ A warm and helpful welcome is of prime importance
◆ Your hairdresser is introduced to you so you can choose your hairstyle together: you won't have a standard haircut.

## THE ART OF SEDUCTION
For this season Jacques Dessange sees you even more seductive than ever: easy maintenance film star style haircuts. Above all, Jacques Dessange's main concern is the well-being of the modern and active woman: the success of the 'Tousled Look' invented by Jacques Dessange has been proved worldwide.

# Map of Calais

**English Channel**

Calais Ce
See Page

Ave R Poincare

Digue Gaston Berthe

Bd de General de Gaulle

Rocade Ouest

Blvd du 8 Mai 1945

Citadelle

Ave P de Courbet

rue de Verdun

Train Station

Blvd Jacquard

D940

Auchan Sainsbury

Fort Nieulay

Avenue Roger Salengro

Blvd Leon Gambetta

rue de Toul

rue des Pontinettes

rue de Valenciennes

Boulevard de l'Europe

Cité Europe
Carrefour
Tesco, Oddbins

Eurotunnel

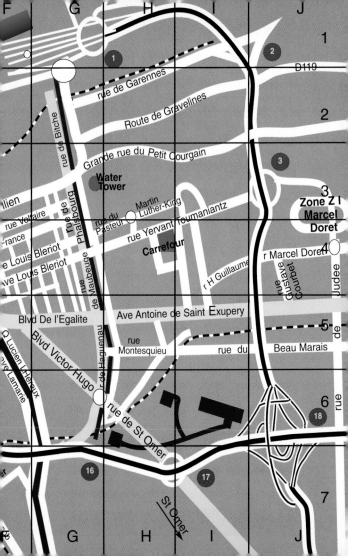

# Auchan Hypermarket

## Auchan Hypermarket
Fort Nieulay, Route de
Boulogne (RN1)
Tel: 00 33 (0)3 21 46 92 92
www.auchan.fr

Map Ref:  B5
Bus No:  5
English:  Yes
Tasting:  Promotion wines only
Payment:  £, 💳 💳
Parking:  Yes
Open:  Monday to Saturday
08.30-22.00
Closed:  Sunday

A uchan Hypermarket's layout makes for easy shopping. It is brightly lit, colourful and spacious. The vast range of wines come predominantly from major French regions with a nod from Portugal, Morocco and Spain. Though there are some fine French wines on the shelves, prices tend to be mainly at the lower end. You can even buy cartons of wine from 40p, such as Ribaudour; don't sniff at this price, they are ideal for cooking.

Sparkling wines are mostly French too. The range of champagnes and beers from around the world, are generally good value.

### How To Get There

**From the ferry** terminal turn left onto the motorway and exit at junction (sortie) 14 following signs to Coquelles and Auchan.

**From Le Shuttle** take the A16 motorway following signs for Calais exit (sortie) 14 then follow signs for Auchan.

### ★ STAR BUYS ★

Clairette de Die £3.15
At last, a good fun fizz offering appealing floral aromas and soft, off-dry, grapey flavours. It's a winner at this price.

Chablis £4.76
This well balanced typically minerally Chablis offers lots of flavour at a very good price.

Castillo de Monovar Reserva 1996 (Spain) £1.70
This red Spanish number has lashings of juicy fruit and a spicy finish - a most enjoyable glug.

Château Le Prat Corbieres 1999 £2.20
A dry and savoury red with a pronounced peppery finish. Lovely with steak.

# Auchan Hypermarket

Saint Nicolas de Bourgueil Le Vendangeoir 1999 £3.30
A red with pure, clean, raspberry aromas, crunchy fruit and strikingly pure fruit.

Nicolas Feuillatte Champagne £9.85
Very good value for this popular easy drinking fizz.

Château Romfort Haut Medoc 1995 £5.50
Interesting, inky, intense aromas. There are no acidic tantrums in this mature and easy drinking wine. Expect softness and a surprisingly dry finish.

## What's On Offer At Auchan? - A Selection
Quantities 75cl unless otherwise shown.

| Sparkling wine | £ |
| --- | --- |
| Pol Remy Brut | 0.70 |
| Pol Remy Muscat Blanc (sweet) | 1.14 |
| Paul Bur Demi Sec | 1.79 |
| Charles Volner | 2.50 |
| Blanquette de Limoux | 2.70 |
| Saumur | 2.70 |
| Café de Paris | 2.75 |
| Kriter | 2.98 |
| Vouvray | 3.00 |
| Aimery | 3.50 |
| Crèmant de Bourgogne St Charles | 3.60 |

| Champagne | £ |
| --- | --- |
| Paul Aime | 6.00 |
| Phillippe de Nantheuil | 6.50 |
| Veuve Emille Brut & Demi Sec | 6.99 |
| Debernard | 7.00 |
| Colligny | 7.38 |
| Philippe de Rezier | 8.99 |
| Jeanmaire | 9.00 |
| Jacquart | 10.00 |
| Alfred Rothschild Brut & Demi Sec | 10.23 |
| Canard Duchêne | 10.90 |
| Duval Leroy | 14.95 |
| Gauthier Brut | 14.95 |
| Lanson Black Label | 12.66 |
| Piper-Heidsieck | 12.73 |
| Mumm Cordon Rouge | 13.50 |
| Laurent Perrier | 14.19 |
| Veuve Cliquot Ponsardin | 16.00 |
| Moët et Chandon Premier Cru | 16.69 |

# Auchan Hypermarket

| Beers | % Vol | £ |
|---|---|---|
| Guinness Special Export 3 x 33cl | 8.0 | 2.64 |
| Munsterbrau 24 x 25cl | 4.7 | 2.85 |
| Heinekin 12 x 25cl | 5.0 | 3.25 |
| Meteor 20 x 25cl | 5.0 | 3.50 |
| Kanterbrau 25 x 25cl | 4.5 | 3.59 |
| 1664 12 x 25 | 5.9 | 3.59 |
| Sterling 24 x 25cl | 4.9 | 3.62 |
| Stella Artois 14 x 25cl | 5.2 | 4.00 |
| 33 Export 24 x 25cl | 4.8 | 4.12 |
| St Omer 24 x 25cl | 5.0 | 4.28 |
| Seumeuse 24 x 25cl | 5.0 | 4.56 |
| Pelforth Blond 20 x 25cl | 5.8 | 4.63 |
| Kronenbourg 24 x 25cl | 4.7 | 5.39 |
| Spitfire Premium Ale 12 x 50cl | 4.5 | 8.50 |
| Bishops Finger 12 x 50cl | 5.4 | 8.90 |
| Shepherd Neame 1698 12 x 50cl | 6.5 | 8.90 |
| Amsterdam Mariner 24 x 50cl | 4.8 | 11.00 |
| Carling Black Label 24 x 50cl | 4.1 | 12.90 |
| Super Crest 24 x 50cl | 10.0 | 13.48 |
| Grölsch 24 x 50cl | 5.0 | 13.60 |
| Fosters 24 x 50cl | 5.0 | 14.00 |
| Tangle Foot 24 x 50cl | 5.0 | 14.00 |
| Bavaria 24 x 50cl | 8.6 | 14.93 |
| Dempseys 24 x 50cl | 4.8 | 15.00 |
| Newcastle Brown Ale 24 x 33cl | 4.7 | 15.00 |
| Bombardier 24 x 50cl | 4.3 | 15.00 |
| John Smith Extra Smooth 24 x 44cl | 4.8 | 16.00 |
| Old Speckled Hen 24 x 33cl | 5.0 | 17.00 |
| Strongbow 24 x 44cl | 5.3 | 17.40 |
| Fosters Ice 24 x 33cl | 5.0 | 17.50 |
| Caffreys 24 x 44cl | 4.8 | 18.60 |
| Kilkenny 24 x 44cl | 5.0 | 19.00 |
| Carlsberg Special Brew 24 x 50cl | 9.0 | 21.40 |
| Gunners 24 x 44cl | 4.1 | 22.00 |

Incidentally
There are also a range of Belgian beers including fruit-flavoured beers on the shelves.

Incidentally
In case you haven't been to Calais for a while, Auchan used to be called Mammouth.

# Carrefour Hypermarket

**Carrefour Hypermarket**
**Cité Europe**
**Coquelles**
Tel: 00 33 (0)3 2146 75 55

Map Ref:    A7
Bus No:     7
English:    Yes
Tasting:    Hold fayres
Payment:    £, 💳 💳
Parking:    Yes
Open:       Monday to Friday
            09.00-22.00 Saturday
            08.30-22.00
Closed:     Sunday

How To Get There

From Calais port turn left onto the A26. Follow the road signed Dunkerque onto A16. Exit junction (sortie) 18, follow signs to Boulogne. Exit at junction (sortie) 12 signposted Cité Europe Ouest. Follow signs to Cité de la Europe, Centre Commercial. You will soon see Cité Europe. Carrefour is on the right (or left depending on where you park) as you enter.

Carrefour hypermarket is a giant dominating the mouth of Cité Europe. It stocks everything and anything at competitive prices. It is bright, colourful, in huge surroundings - so huge that some of the staff get around on roller skates!

There are wines from all areas of France, and a smaller range from the rest of the world. There's also wine in 25cl cartons. A pack of 3 costs 94p, ideal for use in cooking.

Spirits are also available in abundance. The range of beers includes popular Belgian beers and two

heavyweights: The German - **EKU 28** - a 33cl bottle is 85p and a native beer - **La Bière du Demon** - (3 x 33cl £2.63) a pale ale with the inscription *"12% de Plaisir Diabolique"*.

Unfortunately, we were unable to obtain any wines for the annual Channel Hoppers wine tasting this year.

Nevertheless we are confident that Carrefour Hypermarket is an ideal shop stop for general shopping when twinned with Tesco and Oddbins for the wine purchases.

# Carrefour Hypermarket

| Sparkling wine | | £ |
|---|---|---|
| Café de Paris Demi Sec & Brut | | 2.88 |
| Opéra Demi Sec | | 3.01 |
| Kritter Brut de Brut & Demi Sec | | 3.04 |
| Saumur Ackerman Demi Sec | | 3.07 |
| Clairette de Die Brut | | 3.15 |
| Louis de Vernier Blanc de Blancs | | 3.26 |
| Nottage Hill Chardonnay | | 3.67 |
| Vouvray Ackerman Brut | | 4.15 |
| Ackerman Privilege Crémant de Loire | | 4.20 |
| Freixenet | | 4.80 |

| Champagne | | £ |
|---|---|---|
| Vranken | | 9.05 |
| Duval Leroy Brut | | 9.60 |
| de Castellane Brut | | 9.68 |
| Jean Mare Brut | | 9.88 |
| Alfred Rothschild Demi-Sec | | 9.99 |
| Fleury | | 10.00 |
| Charles Cazenove | | 10.57 |
| Gauthier | | 11.21 |
| Demoiselle Vranken | | 12.02 |
| Piper Heidsieck | | 12.04 |
| Lanson Brut | | 12.36 |
| Germain Brut | | 12.52 |
| Mumm Cordon Rouge | | 13.54 |
| Canard Duchêne | | 13.67 |
| Perrier Jouet | | 13.67 |
| Pommery | | 13.89 |

| Beer | % Vol | £ |
|---|---|---|
| La Facon 24 x 25cl | 4.9 | 3.15 |
| Mezbrau 24 x 25cl | 5.0 | 3.36 |
| Heinekin 12 x 25cl | 5.0 | 3.63 |
| Kalbrau 24 x 25cl | 5.0 | 3.57 |
| Strasbrau 24 x 25cl | 4.5 | 3.68 |
| Carrefour Biere Blonde 24 x 25cl | 4.5 | 3.87 |
| 33 Export 24 x 25cl | 4.8 | 4.30 |
| Seumeuse 24 x 25cl | 5.0 | 4.41 |
| Kronenbourg 26 x 25cl | 4.7 | 5.39 |
| St Omer 24 x 50cl | 5.0 | 8.42 |
| Warsteiner 24 x 33cl | 4.8 | 16.78 |
| Caffreys 24 x 24cl | 4.8 | 16.85 |

# Sainsbury's

Sainsbury's
Fort Nieulay, Route de
Boulogne (RN1)
Tel: 00 33 (0)3 21 82 38 48
www.sainsburys.co.uk/calais

Map Ref: B5
Bus No: 5
English: Yes
Tasting: Yes
Payments: £, 💳 💳
Parking: Yes
Open: Monday to Saturday
08.30-21.00
Closed: Sunday

How To Get There

**From the ferry** terminal
turn left onto the motorway
and exit at junction (sortie)
14 following signs to
Coquelles and Auchan
Sainsbury's.

**From Le Shuttle** take the
A16 motorway following
signs for Calais exit (sortie)
14 then follow signs for
Auchan Sainsbury's.

## BEST VALUE CROSS-CHANNEL OFF-LICENCE

SPECIAL OFFER:
Spend over £20 and
get a **Free** bottle
of wine.

Sainsbury's have recently moved to bigger premises, on the same estate, now located outside the Auchan commercial centre. The extra space has made room for a beer range which includes continental and the popular Belgian beers, spirits and a new international fine wine section. In general their products offer good value for money, especially their own branded products such as their Moscatel and superb value Brouilly. There are no rock bottom cheapies to be found, though. According to Sainsbury's wine buyer, Nico Thiriot, "There are many cheap wines in Calais, and there are as many bargain wines. Go for the bargain wines, then you can actually enjoy your wine and you won't wake up with a thumping head in the morning." We'll drink to that. Here are some to try:

# Sainsbury's

Sainsbury's Moscatel De Valencia £1.40
Fresh and grapey, an absolute steal at this price for those who like a traditional style Moscatel.

Bordeaux de Ginestet 1999 £2.75
Smoothy oak aromas, lots of oaky flavour, and sprightly characters.

Château Tassin 1999 Premierès Côtes de Bordeaux £2.80
Though this red is a little light, it's dry and pleasantly flavoured for early drinking

Sainsbury's Muscadet Sèvre et Maine Sur Lie 1999 £2.99
A sprightly white, zippy, clean and bone dry. Ideal with seafood.

Sainsbury's Cava Rosé £2.99
Pleasant enough rosé fizz at a very good price.

Rioja Crianza 1997 Bodegas Olarra £2.99
This Spanish red has soft, sweet fruit, dry finish, and typical Rioja characters at a good price.

Sanctuary Marlborough Chardonnay 1999 £3.40
A decent wine offering mouthfuls of buttery, tropical fruit.

1998 Rosemount Estate Semillon Chardonnay £4.11
Appealing aromas and citrus on the palate.

Los Robles Carmenere £3.20
Lovely vivid colour and bold, fruit of the forest aromas. Crunchy sweet fruit and highly flavoured. This is well rounded red wine and good value for money.

Trapiche Cabernet Sauvignon Oak Cask 1997 £3.99
Bold, classic cabernet aromas, with a touch of cedar and oak. It has opulent flavours and a touch of class.

Sainsbury's Classic Selection Brouilly 1999 £4.50
Vivid youthful colour and delightfully fresh raspberry and pear aromas. Lifted, crunchy fruit, vibrant and irresistible. A delicious wine and a firm favourite with everyone and excellent value.

# Sainsbury's

## What's On Offer At Sainsbury's? - A Selection

Quantities 75cl unless otherwise shown. The first colum is the price in the Calais store. The second column is the UK price.

| Sparkling Wine | £ | UK.£ |
|---|---|---|
| Sainsbury's Cava Rosado | 2.99 | 4.99 |
| Asti Martini | 3.49 | 4.99 |
| Hardys Stamp Chardonnay Pinot Noir Brut | 3.49 | 5.99 |
| Veuve de Vernay | 3.49 | 5.99 |
| Freixenet Cava Rosado Brut | 3.99 | 6.99 |
| Freixenet Cordon Negro Cava | 4.49 | 6.99 |
| Jacob's Creek Special Cuvée | 4.59 | 6.99 |
| Montana Lindauer Brut | 4.98 | 7.49 |
| Banrock Station Sparkling Shiraz | 5.49 | 7.99 |
| Mumm Cuvée Napa Brut | 7.99 | 10.99 |

| Champagne | £ | UK.£ |
|---|---|---|
| Sainsbury's Champagne Blanc de Noirs Brut | 8.99 | 11.99 |
| Sainsburys Champagne Demi Sec | 9.95 | 13.99 |
| Sainsbury's Vintage Champagne | 10.50 | 15.99 |
| Sainsbury's Champagne Rosé Brut | 11.99 | 14.99 |
| Lanson Black Label | 13.99 | 20.99 |
| Piper Heidsieck Brut | 12.80 | 18.99 |
| Mumm Cordon Rouge | 15.40 | 19.49 |
| Veuve Clicquot Brut | 15.99 | 25.48 |
| Moët et Chandon Brut Imperial | 16.49 | 19.49 |

| Beer | % Vol | £ | UK.£ |
|---|---|---|---|
| Cruiser 24 x 25cl | n/a | 3.00 | 7.99 |
| Seumeuse 24 x 25cl | | 3.40 | 8.99 |
| Grölsch 24 x 25cl | 5.0 | 7.99 | 13.49 |
| Amsterdam Mariner 24 x 50cl | 5.0 | 9.99 | 14.99 |
| Carling Black Label 24 x 50 cl | 4.1 | 11.99 | 17.95 |
| Rolling Rock 24 x 33cl | 5.0 | 11.99 | 24.99 |
| Stella Artois 24 x 50cl | 5.2 | 12.16 | 26.16 |
| John Smiths Extra Smooth 24 x 44cl | 4.0 | 12.90 | 18.99 |
| Becks 24 x 33cl | 5.0 | 13.86 | 21.36 |
| Miller 24 x 33cl | 4.7 | 13.99 | 24.99 |
| Guinness Original 24 x 44cl | 4.3 | 14.90 | 21.98 |
| Boddingtons 24 x 44cl | 3.8 | 14.99 | 24.99 |
| Fosters Export 24 x 50cl | 5.0 | 14.99 | 24.99 |
| Tanglefoot 24 x 50cl | 5.0 | 14.99 | 24.99 |
| Holsten Pils 24 x 50cl | 5.5 | 15.99 | 25.99 |
| Caffreys 24 x 44cl | 4.8 | 17.99 | 26.99 |
| Fosters Ice 24 x 33cl | 5.0 | 17.99 | 24.99 |
| Old Speckled Hen 24 x 33cl | 5.0 | 17.99 | 25.99 |
| Guinness Draught 24 x 50cl | 4.2 | 18.99 | 26.99 |
| Carlsberg Special Brew 24 x 50cl | 9.0 | 19.94 | 35.34 |

# Tesco Supermarket

## Tesco

Cité Europe, Coquelles
Tel: 00 33 (0)3 21 460270
www.Tesco.com/vinplus

Map Ref: A7
Bus No: 7
English: Yes
Tasting: Sporadically
Payment: £, [card symbols]
Parking: Yes
Open: Mon-Sat 09.00-22.00
Closed: Sunday

## BEST CROSS-CHANNEL DRINKS SUPERMARKET

Tesco is situated on the lower level of Cité Europe. In true supermarket style Tesco is brightly lit and well laid out. They complement this with the very British "car service" whereby you can obtain your purchases later from the collection point. This is a blessing leaving you to tour the rest of Cité Europe unburdened with heavy shopping. Also instore, you will find possibly the largest range of decent New and Old World wines in Calais in all the price ranges. Alongside more than 700 wines there is a vast selection of beers and spirits making Tesco overall an excellent one-stop drinks supermarket

### How To Get There

From the port turn left and continue onto the A26 motorway. Follow signs to Dunkerque onto the A16 motorway. Exit at Junction (sortie) 18 and follow signs to Boulogne. Exit at Junction (sortie) 12. Follow signs to Cité de la Europe, Centre Commercial. Tesco is on the lower level.

### ⭐ STAR BUYS ⭐

French Connection 2000 Grenache Sauvigon Blanc £1.90
A simple, yet decent gluggy white wine.

Chilean Chardonnay Reserve 2000 £3.30
Ripe peachy fruit here, plenty of flavour, nice fruity oak and crisp fresh quality.

Tesco Australian Chardonnay £2.59
Full on fruit salad flavours of apples, melons, lychees and especially peach and pineapple. Easy to drink.

French Connection 2000 Grenache Syrah £2.00
Warm, scented, almost violets on the nose. Refreshing, chewy fruit and fresh finish. Best with food.

# Tesco Supermarket

Côtes du Rhône Villages 1999 Le Grand Retour £2.00
Reserved aromas, spice in the background. Firm fruit, but may well need another 12 months to show its best. Well priced.

Vintage Claret Bordeaux Supérieur 1997 £2.80
Ripe black fruit aromas, sweet oak in the background. Full bodied for this level of claret, pleasantly highly flavoured, with a long finish.

Tesco Chilean Cabernet Sauvignon £2.90
Pure, ripe cassis aromas. Sweet juicy fruit on the palate, dry finish. A good example.

Terramater Chilean Cabernet Sauvignon 1999 £3.50
Rich, warm, ripe cassis nose, with oaky tones in the background. Sweet, pure blackcurrant fruit, packed with flavour, finishes clean and dry.

Tesco Marlborough Sauvignon Blanc £3.80
Lots of gooseberry zing with a fresh quality, pleasantly juicy and with a good varied character.

Tesco St Emilion 1999 £5.35
This full bodied red has bold, sweet aromas - surprisingly hedonistic for a claret! Rich flavours, attractively round and supple and already drinking well.

Vina Mara Rioja Gran Reserva 1994 £7.00
Classic mature Rioja aromas of nuts and dried fruits, which are still surprisingly vibrant. Great freshness of flavour, full of fruit, and finishing with a grip that suggests it will still improve.

# Tesco Supermarket

## What's On Offer At Tesco? - A Selection

Quantities 75cl unless otherwise shown.

| Sparkling Wine | £ |
|---|---|
| Pol Rémy Brut & Demi-Sec | .70 |
| Moscato Spumante | 1.00 |
| Tesco Asti Martini | 3.20 |
| Crémant d'Alsace Cuvée 2000 | 3.30 |
| Angas Brut both Rosé & White | 3.39 |
| Jacob's Creek Chardonnay/Pinot Noir | 3.45 |
| Sparkling Saumur | 3.90 |
| Seaview Brut | 4.00 |
| Lindauer Brut | 4.70 |
| Cuvée Nappa Mumm Brut | 6.90 |

| Champagne | £ |
|---|---|
| Charles de Cazanove | 8.95 |
| Nicolas Feuillate Brut | 9.50 |
| Gauthier | 10.43 |
| Alfred Rothschild | 10.80 |
| Lanson Black Label | 12.50 |
| Piper Heidsieck | 13.00 |
| Charles Lafitte 1989 | 15.50 |
| Mumm Cordon Rouge | 15.50 |
| Demoiselle Millésime 1994 | 16.00 |
| Moët et Chandon | 16.00 |
| Veuve Cliquot Yellow Label | 16.20 |
| Charles Heidsieck | 16.57 |
| Bollinger | 20.00 |

| Beer | % Vol | £ |
|---|---|---|
| Kanterbrau 24 x 25cl | 4.7 | 4.30 |
| Grölsch 24 x 25cl | 5.0 | 6.50 |
| Amsterdam Mariner 24 x 50cl | 5.0 | 9.00 |
| Kronenbourg 1664 24 x 50cl | 5.9 | 10.80 |
| Bombardier 24 x 50cl | 4.3 | 11.80 |
| Labatt Ice 24 x 33cl | 5.6 | 11.80 |
| Stella Artois 24 x 50cl | 5.2 | 11.90 |
| Fosters Export 24 x 50cl | 5.0 | 12.00 |
| Tanglefoot 24 x 50cl | 5.0 | 12.00 |
| Nastro Azzura 24 x 33cl | 5.2 | 12.00 |
| John Smiths Extra Smooth 24 x 44cl | 4.0 | 12.50 |
| John Smiths Bitter 24 x 50cl | 4.0 | 13.00 |
| Becks 24 x 33cl | 5.0 | 13.90 |
| Fosters Ice 24 x 33cl | 5.0 | 15.00 |
| Becks 24 x 50cl | 5.0 | 16.50 |
| Boddingtons 24 x 44cl | 3.8 | 17.50 |
| Caffreys 24 x 44cl | 4.8 | 17.90 |
| Tennents 24 x 50cl | 9.0 | 18.50 |
| Guinness Draught 24 x 50cl | 4.2 | 19.20 |

# Bar A Vins

Bar A Vins
52 Place D'Armes
62100 Calais

Tel: 00 33 (0)3 21 96 96 31

| | |
|---|---|
| Map Ref: | D3 |
| Bus No: | 7 |
| English: | Yes |
| Tasting: | On request |
| Payment: | £, 💳 💳 |
| Parking: | Yes |
| Open: | Monday-Saturday |
| | 09.00-19.00 |
| | Sunday 09.30-15.00 |
| Closed: | Wednesday |

Is there anyone in Calais more enthusiastic about selling quality French wines than Luc Gille? Luc and his wife Isabel are the team that make this petite, quaint wine shop so adorable. Luc bubbles with passion as he enthuses about the wines he has personally selected at the vineyard. He has spent 14 years in the business so you can be confident of a personal service and meaningful advice.

### ✩ STAR BUYS ✩

Domaine Deshenrys Vin de Pays des Cotes de Thongue 1999 £2.90
A fresh, vibrant red wine with a surprising depth of flavour and grip at this price.

### How To Get There

From the port turn right. At the second roundabout take the third exit (left) towards centre ville. At the end turn right into rue Molien. At the roundabout (Town Hall on left) turn right. At the traffic lights turn right into Place D'Armes.

## BEST PERSONAL SERVICE IN CALAIS

Domaine Masclaux Côtes du Ventoux 1999 £2.95
A lovely red with lots of juicy fruit, brambly characters, spicy finish. Good value.

Côte du Rhône Alain Jaume 1999 £4.40
A well made, ripe, white wine exuding apples, pears and floral scents. It has fine fruit quality, fresh spritz and excellent fruit flavours. It has a great aftertaste too. Excellent!

Quincy Domaine de Chevilly 1999 £4.50
Sancerre look alike white wine with pure sauvignon aromas and a crisp dry finish.

# Bar A Vins

Vire-Clesse 1999 Earl
Rongier £4.60
Ripe, stylish, buttery white.
Good value white wine.

Château Armandière
Cahors 1999 £4.00
Attractive vivid colour and
brooding black fruit aromas.
Mouth filling fruit, cherry
tones, with long length.

Côtes du Rhône Domaine
Grand Veneur 1999 £4.40
Savoury, spicy aromas and
rich flavours so typical of
top wines from the Rhône
valley with all the
characteristics of a more
expensive wine.

Domaine du Grand Cres
Corbières 1999 £4.50
A big, chewy red wine,
pleasing enough, but very
dry at the end. It needs to
be drunk with food.

Domaine de Villargeau
Côteaux du Giennois,
Thibault 1999 £4.80
The pale colour of this red
wine belies the ripe
strawberry aromas with an
explosion of crunchy fruit
flavour on the palate.
Vibrant and very good.

Château de Biran
Pecharmant 1998 £5.10
Intriguing, smoky, lightly
scented aromas, full of
character. Rich cherry and
plum flavours, full bodied.
Needs some good rich
food.

Côtes de Bourg Château
L'Hospital 1999 £5.80
Youthful in colour and on
the nose, it has great purity
of blackcurrant fruit and is
most enjoyable. Intended
for drinking young.

Lussac St Emilion Château
Gaboriat 1997 £5.90
Mature, sweet, stewed
plum aromas. Still plenty
of flavour, but soft and now
fully mature.

Petit Chablis 1999 Alain
Gautheron £5.90
An enjoyable example at a
very reasonable price.

Côte du Jura 1998
Domaine Veuve Parrot et
Fils £6.70
Rich, nutty aromas escape
from this white. Dry, richly
flavoured, with a salty
finish. Highly distinctive,
hugely enjoyable.

# Boozers

Boozers
RN43
Route de Saint Omer
62100 Calais
Tel: 00 33 (0)3 21 19 17 17
www.boozers-calais.com

Map Ref: H7
Bus No: -
English: Yes
Tasting: Yes
Payment: £, VISA ●●
Parking: Yes
Open: 07.00-22.00
daily

### How To Get There

**From the port** turn left and take the A26 motorway (direction Paris) and onto A16 intersection (direction of Boulogne), take 1st exit (sortie 17) - St Omer.

**From the tunnel;** Take A16 motorway in the Calais/Dunkerque direction and exit at junction 17 towards St Omer. Boozers is situated at the next junction.

Boozers almost salutes you as you drive along the A16 motorway. You cannot miss its huge neon sign and slogan "the spirit of Calais".

The interior is bright, well groomed, nicely decorated with a friendly atmosphere especially around the wine tasting bar.

Their product range, overseen by the new manager, ex-chef Stuart Creed, includes a fine range from Bellefontaine. All the colours in this wine range proved a hit with the tasters. Other products include a range of beers,

spirits and mineral water.

Though their best selling wine is their amusingly labelled house wine Frog's Piss at £1.99 we have suggested here a selection of more soberly named but no less palatable alternatives.

## FREE WINE!

Spend £10 or more and take your till receipt and your Channel Hoppers Guide to the tasting bar to receive a bottle of our celebrated Cuvée Patron (red or white) absolutely **FREE**.

# Boozers

★ STAR BUYS ★

**Syrah 1999 Vin de Pays d'Oc Bellefontaine £1.99**
A wonderfully evocative southern French red, scented and richly flavoured with black berry juiciness. What a bargain!

**Merlot 1999 Vin de Pays d'Oc Bellefontaine £1.99**
The wine shows remarkable quality at the price, showing soft ripe juicy blackcurrant fruit. Good value wine.

**Sauvignon 1999 Vin de Pays d'Oc Bellefontaine £1.99**
Another good one from the Bellefontaine range. This one has a lovely flavour and so is very easy to drink. An enjoyable white.

**Petit Chablis 1999 Gerard Tremblay £4.49**
If you like it green apple crisp and sharp, this one is for you.

**Premières Côtes De Blaye 1998 Château Prieure Malesan £ 4.99**
Good quality Bordeaux, with plenty of fruit complementing the oak flavours.

**Saint Romain 1998 Chartron et Trebuchet £8.99**
An attractive modern white wine. Rich honeyed aromas and plenty of fruit, flavour and character. Good value for a decent Burgundy.

**Pessac Leognan 1998 Le Prelat de Pape Clement £9.99**
This ripe, rich, red gives off tobacco aromas and very nice vanilla oak characters. It is full flavoured, quite classy and reasonable value.

# Le Chais Wine Merchant

Le Chais
40 rue de Phalsbourg,
62100 Calais
Tel: 00 33 321978857

Map Ref:  G4
Bus No:  2
English:  A little
Tasting:  Some
Payment:  £, 💳 💳
Parking:  Yes
Open:  09.00-19.00 daily
Closed:  12.00-14.00 daily

Established in 1865 Le Chais warehouse, flanked by two giant wine bottles, has the accolade of being the oldest and most established French wine merchant in Calais.

## How To Get There

On exiting the port turn right following the sign to Centre Ville. At the roundabout take the second exit. At the end of the road turn left into rue Mollien. At the traffic lights turn right. Continue for 100 yards. Le Chais is on the right within an inlet.

## ★ STAR BUYS ★

Simply Red Côtes du Ventoux Grenach Syrah 1999 £ 2.00
Ripe, aromatic and juicy, good crunchy fruit. Packed with flavour, a terrific bargain at the price. Ideal for parties.

Château Lecusse Gaillac 1999 £ 3.90
Impressive aromas, with rich fruit and cedary notes. Lovely, richly flavoured palate, bold and strong.

Fleurie Domaine des Riottes 1999 £ 5.60
Classic, flowery Beaujolais aromas. Fine, fruity red, loads of flavour, good grip, but nicely rounded overall. Top class Fleurie.

## Cheers
ZI du Beau Marais
199 rue Marcel Doret
Tel: 00 33 (0)3 21 19 77 00

Map Ref: 4J
Bus No: -
English: Yes
Tasting: Some
Payment: £, 💳 💰
Parking: Yes
Open: 09.00-19.00 daily

### How To Get There
Leave the port, turn left onto A26 motorway, take the first exit No. 3 to ZA Marcel Doret. Follow the sign ZI Marcel Doret on the roundabout below the auto-route. After Metro turn left at the roundabout. Cheers is next to the AA compound. Look for the big barrel.

Cheers is a newcomer to Calais, joining its warehouse brethren on the Marcel Doret estate. The huge barrel-shaped doorway distinguishes them.

### ★ STAR BUYS ★

Côtes du Ventoux 2000 £1.45
Simple yet delivers bags of flavour and character.

Château Riffaud Haut Montravel 1999 £2.40
A balanced, medium sweet flavouresome wine. Chilled, it makes a fine aperitif.

Petit Bourgeois Sauvignon 2000 £3.49
Good, zesty Sauvignon with plenty of fruit and a citrusy finish.

Petit Chablis Gerard Tremblay 1998 £3.99
Has all the classic Chablis hallmarks, but at half the price. Top value.

Petit Bourgeois Cabernet 1999 £3.49
Pure black fruit aromas, crisp and dry. Highly enjoyable when chilled.

Siglo Crianza Rioja 1997 Spain £4.99
Sweet, raisiny, dried fruits on the nose. Good example of Rioja, decently priced.

Château Portier Fleurie 1999 Cru Beaujolais £5.99
Fine, full bodied example of Fleurie, plenty of raspberry fruit flavour. Dry and firm on the finish, may still improve for a year or two.

# Eastenders Cash & Carry

**Eastenders**
14 rue Gustav Courbet,
Zone Marcel Doret
Tel: 00 33(0)3 21 34 53 33

Map Ref:    4J
Bus No:     -
English:    Yes
Tasting:    No
Payment:    £, 💳 💳
Parking:    Yes
Open:       24 hours daily

### How To Get There
From the Calais ferry terminal turn left onto the A26 motorway and come off at the first junction you come to, junction (sortie) 3 following the sign to Z A Marcel Doret and continue to the roundabout where you will be able to see Eastenders.

The Eastenders empire has been masterminded by the infamous Dave West. From Romford barrow boy to bootleggers' dream in a mere decade, making Eastenders into a major force in Calais. The outlet is literally a massive warehouse - no frills here - just lots of wines. Marlene, Eastenders' wine buyer, has achieved an amazingly mixed range, starting with the much slated German Leibfraumilch to some fabulous buys. But Dave is insistent that "you shouldn't knock Leibfraumilch'. He preaches that "this wine introduced the masses to wine appreciation in the first place, including myself."

⭐ STAR BUYS ⭐

**Dom Mamede 1999 £1.25**
This Portuguese example is sound, ripe, with juicy fruit, perfectly well made, good at the price.

**Riesling Cave de Sigolsheim 1999 £2.75**
There's a hint of riesling petrol, fresh sweetness and a crisp fresh acidity.

# Eastenders Cash & Carry

Crémant de Bordeaux Brut
Paul Ribes AOC £2.75
Quite pleasant creamy ripe
fizz at an affordable price,
surprisingly good value
party fizz.

E Guigal Côte du Rhône
1997 £ 3.75
Attractive, spicy Côtes du
Rhône. The 1998 is even
better if you can find it.

Pouilly Fumé Domaine
Chatelain 1999 £4.95
Typically Sauvignon with
fresh sprintz, flirty minerally
character and nice fruit.

Clos de Ramage Haut
Medoc 1997 £ 4.95
Inky, classic claret tones at
a decent price for those who
like their reds pretty dry.

Morris Shiraz 1996 £5.95
A rich,sweet, spicy, fruity
wine. Easy drinking.

## What's On Offer At Eastenders? - A Selection
Quantities as shown. Prices in-store are in sterling (£)

| Beer | % Vol | £ |
| --- | --- | --- |
| ESP 20 x 25cl | 5.2 | 3.00 |
| Stella Artois 24 x 25cl | 5.2 | 4.80 |
| Holsten Pils 20 x 25cl | 5.5. | 5.00 |
| ESP 24 x 50cl | 5.2 | 7.50 |
| Stella Artois 24 x 50cl | 5.2 | 9.50 |
| Orangeboom 24 x 50cl | 5.2 | 10.00 |
| Kronenbourg 1664 24 x 50cl | 5.9 | 10.00 |
| ESP 24 x 50cl | 9.2 | 11.00 |
| Rolling Rock 24 x 33cl | 5.0 | 11.00 |
| Becks 24 x 33cl | 5.0 | 11.00 |
| Frosty Jack 24 x 50cl | 7.5 | 11.50 |
| Fosters Export 24 x 50cl | 5.0 | 11.50 |
| Labatt Ice 24 x 33cl | 5.6 | 11.50 |
| Miller 24 x 33cl | 4.7 | 13.50 |
| Beamish Black 24 x 50cl | 4.1 | 13.50 |
| Grolsch 24 x 50cl | 4.7 | 13.95 |
| Newcastle Brown Ale 24 x 50cl | 4.7 | 13.95 |
| Tennents 24 x 50cl | 9.0 | 14.50 |
| Carlsberg Special Brew 24 x 50cl | 9.0 | 16.50 |

# Franglais Beer & Wine

Franglais Beer & Wine
CD 215, 62185
Frethun
Tel: 00 33 (0)3 21 85 29 39

| | |
|---|---|
| Map Ref: | Off the map at A7 |
| Bus No: | - |
| English: | Yes |
| Tasting: | Yes, extensive |
| Payment: | £, 💳 💳 |
| Parking: | Yes |
| Open: | Daily 09.00-19.00 |
| | Sat 09.00-18.30 |
| Closed: | Sun 09.30-18.00 |

## How To Get There

On exiting the port turn left onto A16-A26 motorway towards Paris-Reims. Continue to the autoroute to the A16 intersection. Take the A16 signposted Boulogne. Continue to exit (sortie) 11 signposted Gare TGV. Leave the autoroute and turn left over the bridge (D215). Franglais is 900 yards ahead on the right.

## THE BEST CROSS-CHANNEL WINE TASTING FACILITY

Franglais' wine tasting facility is second to none. Olivier, the young, dynamic manager explained why he invested so much in the state-of-the-art Bar A Vin (wine bar) dispenser: "All the wines in the Bar A Vin are individually stored at optimum temperature. This means the wine is tasted at its best. Some outlets offer wine tasting but wines are left open all day so the customer gets a mouthful of vinegar.'

# Franglais Beer & Wine

Olivier is keen to ensure customers get every opportunity to buy wines they like and the staff are happy to impart expert advice. The range of 300 wines include the humble at 94p to Grand Crû Classé wines from Bordeaux and wines to lay down.

★ STAR BUYS ★

Cahors Pierre Sèche 1998 £2.25
A good, savoury, dry Cahors. Very good at the price.

Château Haut Peyruguet Bordeaux 1999 £2.33
Soft, surprisingly fruity for a Bordeaux, ideal for current drinking.

Beaumes de Venise Côtes du Rhône Villages 1999 £2.81
Good, bold, spicy red, plenty of flavour, best drunk young while still fresh and vibrant.

Château Maurine Bordeaux 1996 £3.93
Very classy Bordeaux at the price, with good flavour and underlying oak. Well balanced, will still improve for two to three years.

Castillo de Molina Lontue Chule Cabernet Sauvignon 1999 £4.00
Intense, sweet fruit, richly flavoured, not for those who like their reds bone dry.

Saumur Champigny Couly Dutheil Les Chassoirs 1999 £4.39
Lovely pure, scented fruit, raspberry. Youthful, refreshing and delicious lightly chilled.

Château L'Hospitalet La Clape 1998 Coteaux de Languedoc £5.53
Amazingly classy wine at the price. The oak ageing gives added depth to a wine that already has plenty of character. A bargain.

Château Prieure Malesan Cru Bourgeois 1998 £5.75
Good quality Bordeaux, with plenty of fruit complementing the oak flavours.

Crozes Hermitage Les Jalets P Jaboulet 1998 £5.85
A really top class Crozes Hermitage from a quality vintage. Very fine now, but will still improve.

# Hoverstore

Hoverstore
Calais terminal and on
board Superseacat
Tel: 01304 865000
www.hoverspeed.com

Map Ref:   G1
Bus No:    2
English:   Yes
Tasting:   Yes
Payment:   £, 💳💳
Parking:   Outside
Open:      Daily

Those travelling with Hoverspeed will have the opportunity to shop at the Hoverstore. If you pre-order wines, beers, spirits or fragrances on-line or by telephone you can take advantage of the Select & Collect service. There is certainly lots to recommend:

### ★ STAR BUYS ★

**Bellefontaine 1999 Merlot Vin de Pays D'Oc £1.99**
An uncomplicated French red, dry with good plummy flavours and surprisingly well rounded and supple. Good value.

**Sacred Hill Colombard Chardonnay 1999 £2.25**
Fresh, juicy dry white with plenty of flavour and a softness that makes it easy to drink on its own.

**Blossom Hill £2.49**
An easy drinking casual or party wine.

**Bellefontaine 1999 Chardonnay Vin de Pays D'Oc £2.49**
Pure, nutty aromas, plenty of fruit, bold flavours and a persistent finish. Great value.

**Barramundi Shiraz Merlot £2.49**
Bold, fruity flavours with underlying spicy tones. Plenty of flavour at the price.

**Hardy's Nottage Hill Chardonnay 1999 £2.99**
Delicious, typically Oz Chardonnay with ripe melon flavours and lots of zest and length.

**Nekeas Tempranillo Merlot 1998 £2.99**
This one offers pleasant sweetish fruit, softness and easy glugging.

**Sacred Hill Shiraz Cabernet 1999 £2.99**
Ripe, spicy, liquorice aromas. Strong, bold and richly flavoured. Good value.

**Hardy's Nottage Hill Cabernet Sauvignon Shiraz 1999 £3.49**
Wonderful depth of flavour, brimming with blackcurrant fruit, and sweet, spicy tones. Drink now. A bargain.

**Crozes-Hermitage Vicomte de Lignac £3.99**
Good bold fruit, lots of flavour, at a bargain price. Early drinking.

**Bourgogne du Chapitre Jaffelin 1998 £4.99**
Good depth of flavour for a red Burgundy. It has cherry undertones, firm on the finish but needs food. Good value.

**Domaine Laroche Chablis St Martin 1998 £6.75**
Attractive Chablis, with the subtle balance of dryness and fruit flavour.

**Lindauer Special Reserve Brut Sparkling Wine £6.99**
Consistently high quality fizz combining the riper, juicier flavours of the New World with the finesse of the Old.

**Fetzer Syrah 1997 £7.99**
Packed with flavour and with good pure syrah character. The wine is Flavoursome and soft and should be drunk now - preferably with a roast.

**Château La Commanderie St Emilion Grand Cru Cordier 1997**
A well balanced Bordeaux, full of flavour, with the fruit and oak marrying well together. Drinking now.

**Châteauneuf du Pape 1998 Doffonty Remy £8.99**
The wine is full of rich, bold flavours with spicy undertones. It is a good example from a top vintage. Drink now and enjoy this bargain.

**Georges Gardet Champagne £8.99**
Attractive apple fruit in this good value bottle of fizz.

**Royer Champagne £9.99**
There is lots of quality apple fruit in this authentic and somewhat rustic bottle of bubbly.

# 12 for 11

## on all wines when you buy online

**dovercalais40mins doverostend2hrs
newhavendieppe2hrs**

shop online at www.hoverstore.co.uk and check out hundreds of wines, all at huge savings over uk high street prices. you'll get 12 for the price of 11 on all online wine purchases. then speed across the channel with hoverspeed, and collect your order or browse again in our hoverstores. open 7 days a week, they're conveniently situated right in our terminals in calais, ostend and dieppe.

**for reservations, call 08705 240241**

# www.hoverspeed.com

# hoverspeed

highspeedcarferries

# Intercaves Wine Merchant

**Intercaves**
26 rue Mollien
62100 Calais
Tel: 00 33 321 96 63 82

| | |
|---|---|
| Map Ref: | E4 |
| Bus No: | 2 |
| English: | Yes |
| Tasting: | Yes |
| Payment: | £, 💳 💳 |
| Parking: | Outside |
| Open: | Tuesday - Saturday |
| | 09.30-12.30 and |
| | 14.30-19.30 |
| | Sunday 09.30-12.30 |
| Closed: | Monday and August |

Intercaves describe themselves as "Les Chevaliers du Vins" - the knights of wine! With 100 outlets around France, it seems fairly accurate. This branch specialising in French wine has a pleasant, cosy, non-rushed atmosphere. It is bright, spacious and orderly.

### How To Get There

From the ferry terminal follow signs to Centre Ville (second exit off the roundabout) Continue straight on (railway on the right). At the end turn right into Rue Mollien. Inter caves is 200 yards along on the left hand side close to the traffic lights.

## BEST SELECTION OF BAG-IN-THE-BOX WINES

The wines are rigorously selected from hand picked individual growers and châteaux. Inter caves lay claim to being leaders in vacuumed packed bag-in-the box wines under the Réservavin label. Their selection of around 25 varieties come in 3, 10 and 20 litre tapped cartons which you can try before you buy. Ideal for parties.

★ STAR BUYS ★

Côtes du Ventoux Canteperdrix 1999 £2.57 Appealing, bold aromas, easy to drink and most enjoyable.

# Intercaves Wine Merchant

Jean Marrens Côtes du Marmandais 1998 £3.59
Soft easy drinking style

Château le Grand Buisson Bergerac 1999 £3.70
Bergerac is a sound source of typical claret characters but at a lower price. This is an enjoyable dry red, well worth the money.

Graves Château Roquetaillade Le Bernet 1999 £4.59
Decent quality crisp and refreshing dry white Bordeaux. Good price

Domaine Maby Lirac La Fermade 1998 £4.65
Rustic but quite good sturdy fruit, spicy and robust with some character.

What's On Offer At Intercaves - A Selection

| Red wine boxes | £ |
| --- | --- |
| Vin de Pays d'Oc Marquise des Vignes 10L | 18.30 |
| Vin de Pays Côtes du Tarn Gamay | 18.68 |
| Vin de Pays du Gard Cabernet 10L | 19.45 |
| Côtes du Lubéron AOC 10L | 19.85 |
| Vin de Pays d'Oc Merlot | 19.69 |
| Costières de Nimes AOC 10L | 21.26 |
| Côtes du Frontonnais AOC 10L | 21.85 |
| Côtes du Duras AOC 10L | 26.70 |
| Bergerac AOC 10L | 27.70 |
| Vin de Table Cuvée Fessy 20L | 31.28 |
| Bordeaux AOC 10L | 32.70 |
| Côtes de Bourg AOC 10L | 35.67 |

| Rosé wine boxes | £ |
| --- | --- |
| Vin de Pays du Vaucluse Rosé 10L | 15.50 |
| Vin de Pays du Gard Rosé 10L | 18.30 |
| Côtes du Ventoux AOC Rosé 10L | 20.28 |

| White wine boxes | £ |
| --- | --- |
| Vin de Pays du Vaucluse 10L | 15.50 |
| Côtes du Duras AOC 10L | 18.60 |
| Bergerac Blanc AOC 10L | 20.85 |

There is also an unusual and interesting selection of champagnes available here ranging from £10 to £37. Most have been matured for three years.

# Oddbins Wine Merchant

## Oddbins

Unit 139, Cité de L'Europe
62901 Coquelles
Tel: 00 33 (0)3 21 82 07 32

email: oddbins_calais@oddbins.com

Map Ref:   A7
Bus No:   7
English:   Yes
Tasting:   Some
Payment:   £, 💳💳
Parking:   Yes
Open:   09.00-20.00 daily

## BEST GLOBAL WINE MERCHANT

Oddbins have a petite, delightfully cosy outlet nestling on the lower ground floor of Cité Europe and, perhaps a tad incongriously,, opposite McDonalds. Amazingly, they have managed to cram in about 700 wines from around the globe, at prices well below their UK branches. They are also one of the few stores open on Sunday.

### ☆ STAR BUYS ☆

Price in brackets is the UK price

Scholtzenhof Petit Chenin 2000 £1.70 (£3.99)
It has a pleasantly fresh nose, zest yet both sweet and spicy. An easy drinking bargain party wine.

### How To Get There

From the port turn left and continue onto the A26 motorway. Follow signs to Dunkerque onto the A16 motorway. Exit at Junction (sortie) 18 and follow signs to Boulogne. Exit at Junction (sortie) 12. Follow signs to Cité de la Europe, Centre Commercial until you get to Cité Europe.
Oddbins is on the lower level.

Château Dauliby Bordeaux 1998 £1.98 (£3.99)
Good, sound claret, with attractive, crunchy, youthful flavours and a dry finish. Best drunk young.

Danie De Wet Chardonnay Sur Lie 2000 £2.10 (£3.99)
A pleasant, soft, ripe, buttery Chardonnay with crisp acidity.

Quiltro Cabernet Sauvignon Maipo Valley 1999 £2.20 (£3.99)
Lots of rich, ripe, sweet, blackcurrant flavours, ideal for those looking for an off dry red.

# Oddbins Wine Merchant

Domaine de Molines Sauvignon Voignier Vin de Pays du Gard 1999 £2.40 £4.69)
Nice spicy nose, citrusy, floral fruit, spicy and ripe. Great value.

Dourthe No 1 Sauvignon Blanc 1999 £3.00 (£4.99)
Nice nose, good ripe fruit, clean and delicious fruit. Very good buy.

Tre Uve Ultima £4.00 (£5.99)
A stylish Italian number oozes berry fruit juices, a touch of spice and a delicate lengthy finish. A bargain.

Koonunga Hill Chardonnay 2000 Penfolds £3.50 (£5.99)
A very commercial style but enjoyable nonetheless, especially at this price.

Comte Cathare Fitou 1998 £4.00 (£5.99)
Lightly scented, hints of southern French herbs and spice. Dry, classy and fairly priced.

Errazuriz Estate Merlot 2000 £4.00 (£6.49)
A pleasant wine with sweet minty fruit and quite chocolatey. Needs decanting.

Glorioso Rioja Crianza 1997 £4.60 (£6.99)
"Glorious", rich, sweet aromas, impressive fruit on the palate, richly flavoured, but finishes fresh and dry. A bargain.

E Guigal Côtes du Rhône 1998 £4.99 (£7.49)
Fine deep colour, with sweet brambly aromas showing great purity. Terrific fruit and flavour, highly attractive, top class at the price.

Wither Hills Marlborough Sauvignon Blanc 2000 £5.30 (£7.99)
A fresh nose, classic purple hue and great tropical juicy fruit. Excellent value.

Chablis Jean Marc Brocard 1999 £5.33 (£8.29)
A fresh bouquet, typical dry, mineral characters. A bargain price for a classic.

Seaview Brut 1996 Blanc de Blancs £6.20 (£8.99)
A delicious fruity bottle of fizz. Lots of apples and pears packaged elegantly. Another bargain.

Henri Harlin Champagne £9.38 (14.99)
Ripe apples in a creamy fresh quality. A good buy at the price.

# Perardel Wine Merchant

### Perardel
**A Z Marcel Doret**
**Calais**
Tel: 00 33 (0)3 21 97 21 22

| | |
|---|---|
| Map Ref: | J3 |
| Bus No: | 1 (closest) |
| English: | A little |
| Tasting: | Yes |
| Payment: | £, 💳 |
| Parking: | Yes |
| Open: | 08.15-19.45 daily |
| | Sunday 09.00-19.45 |

How To Get There

Turn left out of Calais port onto the A26 motorway and exit at junction (sortie) 3. At the roundabout take the first exit signposted Zone Marcel Doret. Continue for a quarter of a mile until you see Perardel on the left hand side.

## BEST CROSS-CHANNEL OUTLET FOR THE DISCRIMINATING WINE LOVER

Perardel offers a pleasing mix of wines including a delightful find from Saint Pourcain and a fine, classy red Bordeaux.

In store their top class range includes quality middle-range burgundies, clarets and white wines in £5.00-£10.00 price range. Wines from Alsace and the Loire also feature to a lesser extent. Many French names and vintages are on offer and there are many fine wines in the "sell the silver" price bracket such as Château Lafite for around £60.00 and

**FREE WINE!**

Spend at least £30 and receive a
free bottle
of quality wine.
The more you spend the better quality your free wine will be.

You must show your guide to be eligible.

# Perardel Wine Merchant

Château Latour for around £55.00. Perhaps unsurprisingly there is a large range of champagnes whose number tops 100.

In stark contrast there are some table wines which are sold en vrac (draught).

They now have a range of New World wines, and a range of beers.

If you are tentative about wine, Perardel have a computer on hand which you can use to get a description of any wine that interests you. Alternatively feel free to experiment at the small wine tasting bar.

# Perardel Wine Merchant

Premières Côtes de Blaye, Château Le Grand Moulin 2000 £3.30
Youthful on the nose, with elderflower and black fruits on the palate. It has good, crunchy fruit offering a vibrant, crisp, uncomplicated and enjoyable early drinking.

Bourgogne Aligote 1999 Pérardel £3.90
Bold aromas emanate from this traditional white Burgundian example. The wine offers more flavour than most of its counterparts. A good buy.

Sauvignon De St-Bris William Févre 1998 £4.40
A traditional white Burgundian wine with bold aromas and with more flavour than most of its counterparts.

Crémant de Loire Perardel Perles d'Or £4.90 (£4.60 for six)
A dry earthy mouthful of very easy drinking fizz.

Domaine des Conquêtes Vin de Pays de l'Hérault 1996 £4.80
A mix of southern sun and new oak has created this classy, spicy, bold flavoursome red.

Château du Moulin Rouge 1997 Haut-Médoc Cru Bourgeois £5.80
This traditional style Claret has a medium body and refined flavours which are ideally suited to roast meat.

Châteauneuf-du-Pape 1998 Domaine du Vieux Lazaret 1998 £7.30
This one has fresh fruit cake aromas giving way to a rich, full bodied wine nicely rounded and with lingering length.

Champagne Louis Chesnel Burt Carte D'Or £7.50 (£6.90 each for six)
This youthful, crisp, dry Champagne offers lots of fizz and soft flavours at a bargain price. If you do find it a tad tart turn it into a Bucks fizz or Kir Royale.

# Pidou Cash & Carry

## Pidou
190 rue Marcel Dassault,
Zone Marcel Doret
62100 Calais
Tel: 00 33 3 21 96 78 10

Map Ref:    J4
Bus No:     1 (closest)
English:    Yes
Tasting:    Yes
Payment:    £, 💳 💳
Parking:    Yes
Open:       24 hours

Pidou appears to attract the bulk buyer. Its large car park is laden with trucks and coaches. Not surprising, since it has some attractive facilities such as a spacious car park, coffee machines, currency exchange and even a special check-out for lorry drivers.Shopping includes a souvenir shop, groceries and sandwiches. Outside there is a chippy and a hut selling Belgian chocolates. Inside there is a wide selection of mainly cheap French wines, but they do have a fine selection of beer to entice any passing trucker!

### ★ STAR BUYS ★

**Pol Remi Demi-Sec £0.81**
A party fizz for the youngsters and gives fun corks to pop.

**Gewurztraminer 1999 £3.60**
Lychee flavours to enjoy in a fine example of this wine.

Les Ormes de Cambras Cabernet Sauvignon 1999 £1.90
Good cabernet style on aroma and palate. Soft, round fruit, sound example.

Côtes Rocheuses Saint Emilion Grand Cru 1997 £5.90
Sweet, oaky, dried fruit aromas, soft, mature - nice with roast lamb.

# Pidou Cash & Carry

## What's On Offer At Pidou? - A Selection of beers

| Beer | % Vol | £ |
|---|---|---|
| Blondy 24 x 25cl | 5.0 | 2.95 |
| Nordik Pils 24 x 25cl | 5.0 | 3.00 |
| Blonderbrau 24 x 25cl | 4.6 | 3.30 |
| Magister 24 x 25cl | 5.0 | 3.30 |
| Authentic Strong Beer 24 x 25cl | 5.2 | 3.40 |
| Sullington 24 x 25cl | 6.2 | 3.49 |
| Mariner Long Neck 24 x 33cl | 4.8 | 3.72 |
| Blonde de Lys 24 x 25cl | 4.9 | 3.90 |
| Sphinx 30 x 25cl | 5.4 | 4.00 |
| Kanterbrau 24 x 25cl | 4.7 | 4.73 |
| Kronenbourg 1664 24 x 33cl | 5.2 | 5.40 |
| Grolsch 24 x 25cl | 5.0 | 6.72 |
| Amsterdam Mariner 24 x 50cl | 5.0 | 7.44 |
| Goudale 6 x 75cl | 7.2 | 7.74 |
| Stella Artois 24 x 33cl | 5.2 | 8.69 |
| Brauperle 24 x 50cl | 8.8 | 9.36 |
| Hoegaarden 24 x 25cl | 5.0 | 9.80 |
| Bishops Finger 12 x 50cl | 5.4 | 9.96 |
| San Miguel 24 x 33cl | 5.4 | 9.96 |
| Labatt Ice 24 x 33cl | 5.6 | 10.20 |
| Rolling Rock 24 x 33cl | 5.0 | 10.80 |
| Nastro Azzura 24 x 33cl | 5.2 | 10.80 |
| John Smiths Bitter 24 x 50cl | 4.0 | 11.00 |
| Skona Extra 24 x 50cl | 8.6 | 11.40 |
| Abbaye de Leffe Bonde 24 x 25cl | 6.6 | 11.56 |
| Leffe Brune 24 x 25cl | 6.5 | 11.56 |
| Budweiser 20 x 25cl | 5.0 | 11.60 |
| Stella Artois 24 x 50cl | 5.2 | 12.00 |
| Stones 24 x 50cl | 3.7 | 12.00 |
| Tanglefoot 24 x 50cl | 5.0 | 12.24 |
| Miller 24 x 50cl | 4.7 | 12.40 |
| Bombardier 24 x 50cl | 4.3 | 12.48 |
| Becks 24 x 33cl | 5.0 | 12.50 |
| Heineken 24 x 33cl | 5.0 | 12.60 |
| Carling Black Label 24 x 50 cl | 4.1 | 12.96 |
| Newcastle Brown Ale 24 x 50cl | 4.7 | 13.00 |
| Crest Super 24 x 50cl | 10.0 | 13.20 |
| John Smiths Extra Smooth 24 x 44cl | 4.0 | 13.50 |
| Becks 24 x 50cl | 5.0 | 13.68 |
| Fosters Export 24 x 50cl | 5.0 | 14.00 |
| Fosters Ice 24 x 33cl | 5.0 | 14.00 |
| Holsten Pils 24 x 50cl | 5.5 | 14.00 |
| Boddingtons 24 x 44cl | 3.8 | 14.40 |
| Kestrel Super 24 x 50cl | 9.0 | 15.50 |
| Caffreys 24 x 44cl | 4.8 | 15.60 |
| Beamish 24 x 44cl | 4.2 | 15.60 |
| Budweiser 24 x 33cl | 5.0 | 16.20 |
| Carling Premier 24 x 50cl | 4.7 | 16.80 |
| Tennents 24 x 50cl | 9.0 | 17.76 |
| Warsteiner 24 x 50cl | 4.8 | 18.00 |
| Kronenbourg 1664 24 x 50cl | 5.9 | 18.96 |
| Guinness Original 24 x 44cl | 4.3 | 19.80 |
| Carlsberg Special Brew 24 x 50cl | 9.0 | 20.16 |
| Guinness Draught 24 x 50cl | 4.2 | 22.80 |

# Le Terroir

Le Terroir
29 rue des Fontinettes
Calais
Tel: 00 33 (0)3 21 36 34 66

Map Ref:   E5
Bus No:    16
English:   Yes
Tasting:   Yes
Payment:   £,  💳 💳
Parking:   Street
Open:      Tues to Sat
           09.00-19.30
           Sun 09.30-13.00

Le Terroir is a family-owned business run by the energetic Michel Morvan.

He has created a very pretty shop with a range of French wines starting at just £2. They also sell complementary food items and one of their specialities is making up baskets of their products beautifully wrapped for presenting as gifts. The best part of the shop is located downstairs. As you descend you begin to detect a musty aroma and once on lower ground level you realise you are in an authentic wine cellar complete with dust. Some wines date back to 1876!

---

### How To Get There

From the ferry terminal turn left onto the A16/A26 motorway and exit at junction signposted Calais St Pierre. At the stop, turn right. At the roundabout take 3rd exit in the direction Calais Centre. Continue straight until the second roundabout and take first exit (right) following sign Calais Centre. Continue into rue de Valenciennes. At the end of the road turn left in front of the post-office. The shop is on the left side.

---

### ☆ STAR BUYS ☆

Bordeaux du Cassagne
Bordeaux 1995 £2.50
Refined, stalky aromas. Fully mature, soft, decent Bordeaux character

# Le Terroir

Château Rogue-Peyre 2000 Bergarc £2.59
An elegant raspberry flavoured rosé with a dry finish.

Petit Chablis Gerard Tremblay 1998£ 4.95
This Chablis has all the classic hallmarks. Top value.

Clos de Malte Lalande de Pomerol 1997 £4.99
Ripe, plummy, touch of tobacco on the nose. Rounded, fruity, supple and good example of the appellation.

Château Lagorce Bernadas Moulis en Medoc 1998 £6.95
A lovely nose of lifted cassis aromas, viviid youthful fruit, soft and juicy with creamy oak in the background. A beautifully balanced claret that will last for another two to three years. A real find.

Pouilly-Fumé Marie de Beauregard 1995 £7.50
Lots of quality fruit in this fresh, minerally and complex wine. Very good value.

Sancerre Marie de Beauregard 1995 £7.50
Lots of fruit in this good quality complex wine.

# Wine & Beer Company

The Wine & Beer
Company
rue de Judee
ZA Marcel Doret
Calais
Tel: 00 33 (0)3 21 82 93 64
www.wineandbeer.co.uk

Map Ref:   J4
Bus No:    1 (closest)
English:   Yes
Tasting:   Yes
Payment:   £, 💳
Parking:   Yes
Open:      07.00-22.00 daily

★ STAR BUYS ★

The Wine and Beer Company is a British owned cash & carry and one of two in Calais. This branch is housed in a large warehouse, but without the usual chaos and dust associated with warehouse outlets. The Wine & Beer Company has a spacious, well laid out and fun themed environment in which to shop. Staff are bilingual and can advise on the wines.

The selection consists of around 400 wines from 16 countries offering a variety of styles starting at 89p for 'party' wines.

Primitivo Salento Caleo ·
£1.99
Warm, tarry, characterful at the price, ideal with pasta and a creamy sauce.

Cooper's Block
Chardonnay 1999 £2.49
This easy drinking wine is the Wine & Beer Company's house wine. With tropical fruit in an oak style, the wine is a good introduction to the joys of sunny Oz chardonnay especially at the price.

# Wine & Beer Company

Cooper's Block Shiraz Cabernet Sauvignon1999 £2.99
Simple, cherryish, decent party fodder with residual sweetess and with a deceptive 13% abv.

L A Cetto Petite Syrah 1997 £3.29
Sweet, warm, lightly scented Mexican number with a touch of spice. Very fine. Wonderfully bold flavours, mouth filling and a spicy, long finish. Amazing flavour and even a touch of class at the price.

Marius Reserve 1994 £3.49
Ripe aromas of vanilla and plums, an enticing Spanish wine. Dry fruit, good length of flavour. Dry on the finish, may be better in a couple of years having softened.

Seguret Cotes du Rhône Villages 1998 £3.69
Savoury, sweet aromas, lightly spiced, quite exotic. Juicy, jammy style, lots of flavour with a pleasing finish.

Baron J. De Montfort St Emilion 1999 £3.99
Smoky, dark fruit aromas. Decent fruit and character, dry finish, needs a couple of years.

La Cuvee Mythique Vin de Pays d'Oc 1998 £3.99
Deep colour, ripe, raisiny aromas. Dry, crunchy, ripe fruit, hints of cherries. Crying out for some roast meat for company.

Gewurztraminer 1999 Cuvée des Amoureux £4.49
Typical rose petal aromas, attractively spicy lychee fruit with touch of sweetness.

Chartron et Trebuchet Bourgogne 1998 £5.29
Easy drinking, light medium-bodied red Burgundy.

James Halliday Griffith Botrytis Semillon 1996 £5.69 half bottle.
Ripe, forward, honeyed tones with luxurious apricot characters. Delicious on palate, sweet and balanced.

Trinity Hill Sauvignon Blanc 2000 £5.99
Lots of good New Zealand fruit on the palate.

# What is Cité Europe?

**With representation from every European country, you instantly become an international shopper just by walking through the doors of Cité Europe!**

Cité Europe is located in the village of Coquelles in Calais. Just a decade ago - prior to the development of Eurotunnel and Cité Europe - the area was simply a village road.

The name Coquelles is thought to be of Latin origin. deriving from the name of Eustache de Kalquella, who in 1183 was the first lord or Coquelles. At that time the village, just a mere hamlet, was situated near the old tower remains of the 13th-century church of Old Coquelles. Since then the area has had a series of European occupants: first the Romans, then the English for more than two centuries, the Spanish for a mere two years and the Germans for four years. How apt that Cité Europe should be built on this very European site.

The philosophy behind Cité Europe is to bring to the shopper a truly cosmopolitan choice of shops. Each European country is represented in this immense indoor shopping centre.

Some 59,000 square metres on two levels is home to 11 major stores, including a hypermarket and 150 shops selling everything you can imagine from all over Europe. Familiar names include the **Body Shop**, **Etam**, **Tesco**, **Tie Rack**, **Toys R Us**, **Kokai** and **Naf Naf**.

# What is Cité Europe?

Stylish, casual wear is available at **Aigle** (highly regarded in France), **Zara** and **Carbonne**. For trendy kids clothes visit **Catimini** and **Petit Boy** and for shoes step into **Nikita K** and **Salamander**.

You may also want to dress your home. Whether you wish to add beauty with enchanting crystal, enhance your wine and dining experience with impressively designed porcelain and crockery or adorne your dining room with chic and unusual tablewear, then a trip to Geneviève Lethu is highly recommended. This chain of shops is named after its founder who opened her first shop in 1972. She was the first in France to sell everything associated with dining under one roof. So popular were her exclusive designs that the business developed into a chain of 45 stores world-wide. Sadly, the UK does not have a store, so shop here for wedding presents or for yourself while you can.

We have a selection of over 1000
?hampagnes,wines,spirits and beers,for all your
wedding / party needs.

?offer :

?re-ordering facility

?roduct tastings

?uge selection of new world wines

?ine advice from a trained specialist

?ell known and familiar products

?nglish speaking staff

?ayment in sterling if required

?mple parking

?arry to car service

?LUBCARD POINTS on purchases

?0 shops and restaurants in the

?te Europe complex.

?e us with any questions you may have, for
?tions, or for a copy of our price list, on
?3 321 460 270 or fax on 00 33 321 460 277

# What is Cité Europe?

Shopping is certainly the main event in Cité Europe, but it is essential to find somewhere to rest your weary feet and enjoy delicious food.

Head for the myriad of restaurants on the lower level. The dining area offers everything from sauerkraut to pizzas and hamburgers from the omnipresent McDonald's. There's even a pub where you can enjoy a pint or two.

Some parts of the dining area have been designed in the style of the respective country so as to enhance the international flavour and ambience.

Leisure is also considered an important aspect of Cité Europe. With this in mind Cité Europe also has a 12-screen cinema complex to accommodate all viewing preferences.

For the kids there is an adventure playground, a merry-go-round, simulators and a variety of video games.

And finally, not forgetting the wine, beers and spirits, you can enjoy a wonderful shopping day out and still go home with alcoholic bargains from Carrefour Hypermarket, Tesco Supermarket, Oddbins or Le Chais.

---

**How To Get There**

Cité Europe is situated opposite Eurotunnel, ideal for those travelling via the tunnel.

From Calais port, turn left as you come out and join the A26 Autoroute. Then join the A16 Autoroute following signs to Boulogne exiting at Junction 12 (sortie 12).

Bus Route No: 7
Calais Map Ref: A7

---

DAY TRIPPERS BEWARE!
A visit to Cité Europe is a day trip in itself.
Once there you will find it very difficult to leave.

*C*ome to Nord-Pas-de Calais and be entranced by the diverse landscapes in the Avesnois and Flanders and by the many sporting activities: sand yachting, horse riding, cycling, windsurf, flysurf and golf.

*Let's take a stroll along stunning beaches and explore miles of wild Opal coastline. Or make a rendez-vous with history and art in one of the many local museums and historic sites dotted around the various cities such as Lille, Boulogne Sur Mer, Arras, Cambrai, St Omer... or enjoy the peaceful tranquility of the marsh land in the Audomarais. Why not try the local specialities and gourmet dishes, traditional flavours and beer, in the heart of a region where good living is an everyday event. No doubt you have been to Nord-Pas de Calais*

*before - once perhaps or many times - for a long or a short stay - but now, in 35 minutes, you could be a million miles away. So what are you waiting for? Come to Nord-Pas de Calais!*

New! The Nord-Pas de Calais on line:
www.northernfrance.tourism.com

*For further information about the Nord-Pas de Calais region, contact us:*

*email: contact@crt-nordpasdecalais.fr*
*Comité Régional de Tourisme Nord-Pas de Calais*
*6 place Mendès, France BP 99, 590028 Lille Cedex, France*

*Tel: 00 33 (0)3 20 14 57 57*
*Fax: 00 33 (0)3 20 14 57 58*

**D940, N1, A16 - are the three different routes from Calais to Boulogne. Which do you take?**

Once, the N1 was considered the main link between Calais and Boulogne. This was superseded by the A16-motorway, enabling a 20 minute dash between the two towns. Parallel to the A16 and N1 is one of the area's best kept secrets - the D940.

This is the scenic coastal route or Corniche de la Côte d'Opale which ambles lazily along the Côte d'Opale. It will get you to Boulogne... eventually. Head towards the harbour and pick it up by the Calais plage (beach) signposted Boulogne par la Côte and head in the direction of Sangatte. This long and winding road takes you through Blériot Plage which has its own claim to fame. It was here in 1909 that the famous aviator Louis

Blériot made his epic first flight across the Channel. The road passes the eight kilometres of sandy beach and over to the undulating chalk hills of the twin headlands, Cap Blanc Nez and Cap Gris Nez where swimmers taking on the Channel come ashore. Take time out here and make your way to their tops for a great visual rhapsody of untamed cliffs, the rugged greenery, the blue of the sky all reflected in the expanse of the sea.

The land at Cap Gris Nez protrudes further out into the Channel making it the closest point to the British Isles. It is also an ideal point for bird watching.

Sandwiched between these headlands are the tiny fishing villages of Escalles and Wissant

In Escalles there's a fabulous panoramic dining opportunity at a family run restaurant called Le Thomé de Gamond perched humbly on the top of Mont Hubert. The restaurant is designed so that diners are always assured a table by the window.

Next door is the Musée de Transmanche, a museum about the various historical attempts to cross the Channel either by air, sea, tunnel or by those who chose to swim! (Open daily from April to September - 10.00-18.00 - closed on Mondays. Entrance fee is around £2.00).

Wissant, a small seaside resort, has been nicknamed by the French as la **Perle Sauvage d'Opale**, the wild pearl of the Opal Coast. Perhaps this is due to its croissant-shaped stretch of white sand. It is also where the fisherman park their boats. You can sometimes see fishermen selling their wares almost straight from the sea. Their fishing boats containing the catch of the day are hauled into the village square and they trade direct from them.

Further along the coast the beautiful fishing village of Audresselles is home to a Hôtel de la Plage, a quaint restaurant. Audresselles still has its old Atlantic Wall fortifications dating from the German occupation. The fisherman here park their flobarts - fishing boats - by their homes alongside their tractors. The flobarts are blessed every year on 15th August -

a ceremony carried out in period costume.

Dotted all along the D940 route are many temptations to lure you to stop and shop. You may see farmers selling their freshly grown fruit and vegetables in open huts. These are usually located by the roadside. Or you may see signs directing you to places where you can buy fresh seafood or flowers.

Further along the D940 are the quaint villages of Ambleteuse and Audinghen. Both these villages are culturally noteworthy as each has its own war museum both of which are worth visting before moving on.

Audinghen is home to a quaint restaurant called L'Estival, housed in a wooden chalet and offering a convivial atmosphere in which to dine. The port at Ambleteuse was built by Vauban, the famous French military engineer. Its museum displays about 100 wartime uniforms.

Situated at the foot of Boulogne, just six miles away, is Wimereux - a beautiful picture postcard seaside resort. Its sandy beaches make Wimereux popular with the French and tourists alike. During the summer the resort is buzzing with families and sunshine seekers.

As well as the promenade and the fine beaches there are pretty streets, winding roads and quaint cafés, restaurants and shops.

Wimereux is also home to Mille Vignes, a quality wine merchant specliasing in French wine.

A few sand dunes later, the D940 finally ends and Boulogne begins......

*Legend has it that in 636 AD a boat carrying only a statue of the Virgin Mary washed up on the beach of Boulogne and made it a pilgrimage site. Now they gather for the fish !*

Boulogne has always been considered a very pleasant stopover, but those staying a little longer can enjoy the beauty, charm and heritage of both the old and new town.

The town itself is laced with quaint streets and shops and if you walk past the tidal harbour as far as the beach to the Sailor's Calvary you will be rewarded with a good view of the port.

If you venture higher up to the old city (vieille ville) you will find the appealing 13th-century ramparts - miraculously unscathed after World War II. They surround a network of narrow cobbled streets where you can find peace from the madding crowds and enjoy a peaceful and romantic walk. The most vibrant street of the old town is rue de Lille, a cobbled pedestrianised road full of shops,

restaurants and wine bars. Boulogne's claim to fame is that it is France's premier fishing port - in fact a quarter of Boulogne's population are involved in fishing. A staggering 60,000 tonnes of fish are auctioned annually, making this the biggest auction in France. Moreover, every year Boulogne celebrates its Fête du Poisson (Fish Festival) during July when 20,000 fish and seafood enthusiasts come to enjoy the grand procession led in spirit by the Virign Mary in her capacity as patron saint of fishermen.

A major attraction is the Nausicaa national sea centre. It is only a few moments from the port with its own restaurant and multi-media library. At Nausicaa you can enjoy the magnificent wonders of the underwater world and experience the interactive terminals to the underwater observation tanks including the shark aquarium. To appreciate the aquatic education available, you

restaurants offering anything from a sandwich to a 3 course meal.

should allow two fascinating hours. In case all that marine watching makes you hungry, Nausicaa also has two

Boulogne has its own nature reserve at the Parc Naturel Regional Boulonnais. The area from the bay of Authie to the Oye beach, some 100km of coastline, is adorned with cliffs, dunes and marshes, and is preserved as a safe haven for birds and plants. Footpaths have been created for visitors and guided tours are organised to discover the national heritage.

Boulogne also has its own forest spanning more than 200 hectares. You can enjoy a ramble through the 13 kilometres of signposted footpaths or if you prefer more exhilaration, try cross-country horse riding. Alternatively you can hire a bicycle for a leisurely pedal through the countryside.

Golfers can tee off at no fewer than three 18-hole golf courses: one at Wimereux and two in Hardelot.

Perhaps a little shopping at one of the hypermarkets or street markets followed by a drink and croissant, is more your style. If so, you will be pleased with the myriad of restaurants and continental style cafés Boulogne has to offer.

---

**How to Get
From the Port to the Town**

Turn right after customs, then right again after the Jean-Baptiste Pierre building, to the traffic lights and turn left. Pass under the flyover, turn left into the slip road to the traffic lights. The seafront is over the bridge - Pont de L'Entente Cordial - and then left. For Boulogne centre cross over the bridge to the Grande Rue - high street.

---

Nausicaä Centre National de la Mer
Bvd Sainte-Beuve Open daily - 10am-6pm. Tel: 03 21 30 99 99

Parc naturel régional du Boulonnais Maison du Parc à le Wast Tel: 03 21 83 38 79

Golf - (all 18 holes)
Golf de Wimereux, route d'Ambleteuse, Wimereux
Tel: 03 21 32 43 20
Golf des Pins
avenue de Golf, Hardelot
Tel: 03 21 83 73 10
Golf des Dunes
avenue Edouard VII Hardelot
Tel: 03 21 91 90 90

Horse Riding Centre Équestre du Boulonnais
Tel: 03 21 83 32 38

Bicycle Hire
Youth Hotel, Rue Porte Gayole
Tel: 03 21 83 32 59

Fish Market
Quai Gambetta Mon. to Sat. mornings. Opp. SeaCat Port.

General Market Days
Place Dalton.
All day Wed & Sat

**Tourist brochures applaud the charm
and beauty of Boulogne,
but is it just a pretty face?**

### Hôtel de Ville,
### Place de la Résistance

The Town Hall has been altered six times since it was restored in the 18th century. It houses oil portrait paintings and the Wedding Room contains wood carvings from Dutch Oak.

### Château-Museé
### rue de Bernet

There is so much to see in this medieval Château Museum you may well run out of time. It was originally built by the Count of Boulogne and his wife Mahaut, and now you can walk through the vaults and underground passages of this listed building. In the museum you can enjoy antique Grecian vases, Egyptian sarcophagi, Renaissance coins, Eskimo and Aleutian masks and many exhibits brought back from Oceania 100 years ago by the sailors of Boulogne.

### Le Belfroi

(attached to the Town Hall) The 12th-century belfry is the oldest monument in the Old Town. It was once used as a dungeon and symbolises communal liberty. It is worth visiting if only for the breath-taking views of the port, the town and the sea. Access is from the ground floor of the Town Hall. Entrance is free.

### Basilique Notre-Dame,
### Enc de l'Evêche

This hybrid cathedral was collectively inspired by St Paul's Cathedral, St Peter's in Rome, the Panthéon and Les Invalides in Paris.

It is located on top of a 12th- century maze of crypts and its dome dominates Boulogne town. It has 14 chambers containing vestiges of the 3rd-century Roman temple and many bejewelled religious artefacts.

### Les Remparts

Did you know that Boulogne is a walled city? Not many do. The 13th-century fortifications surround the cobbled streets of the Haute Ville. Built by the Count of Boulogne on the foundations of a Gallo-Roman wall, it has four gates and seventeen turrets. The fortifications and the castle are the best preserved from that period. in Northern France. Take a peaceful stroll along the ramparts to enjoy the panoramic views of the town and its coastline.

Le Bellfroi

The cathedral dome dominates the town of Boulogne

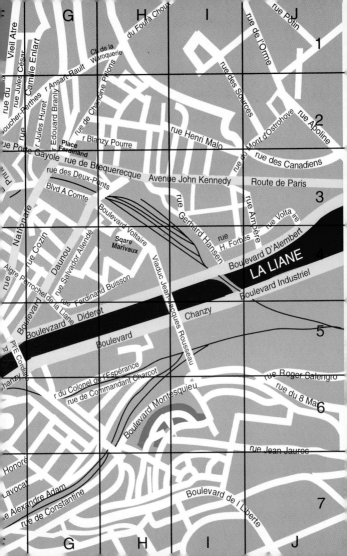

## Auchan Hypermarket

### Auchan
### RN42
### 6220 St-Martin Boulogne

| | |
|---|---|
| Map Ref: | Follow E1 direction |
| Bus No: | 8 |
| English: | No |
| Tasting: | No |
| Payment: | £, 💳 💳 |
| Parking: | Yes |
| Open: | Monday to Saturday 08.30-22.00 |
| Closed: | Sunday |

Auchan Hypermarket is generally considered the biggest and the best place to visit in Boulogne for general supermarket shopping. It is brightly lit, spacious, and colourful.

**How To Get There**

From the port of Boulogne initially follow signs to St Omer and St Martin-B then signs for St Martin B-Centre. Follow the N42 straight through the town on the Route de St Omer and cross over the roundabout with McDonald's on the right. Cross over the next roundabout too, continue for 1.5 miles, take the exit Centre Commercial direct to Auchan and follow signs to Centre Commercial. Auchan will loom up ahead of you.

## Centre E Leclerc Supermarket

### Centre E. Leclerc
### Boulevard Industrial
### de la Liane, 62230 Outreau

| | |
|---|---|
| Map Ref: | Follow J4 |
| Bus No: | 22 |
| English: | No |
| Tasting: | No |
| Payment: | £, 💳 💳 |
| Parking: | Yes |
| Open: | Mon to Sat 09.00-20.00 |
| Closed: | Sunday |

Much like a hypermarket in its style, but intimate enough to be called a Supermarket. Generally,

**How To Get There**

Take A16 from Calais direction Boulogne. Follow the signs to Z I de la Liane on Boulevard Chanzy (alongside the canal on the left). Continue for about a quarter of a mile and Centre E. Leclerc is on the right hand side.

shopping looks like value. Wines are mostly French. Those that are not tend to be a few from Oz.

# Cave Paul Herpe Wine Merchant

## Cave Paul Herpe
85 rue Pasteur,
6220 St Martin Boulogne
Tel 00 33(0)3 21 31 07 15

| | |
|---|---|
| Map Ref: | Follow H5 direction |
| Bus No: | 9 |
| English: | Not much |
| Tasting: | En vrac |
| Payment: | £, 💳 💳 |
| Parking: | Yes |
| Open: | 09.00-19.00 daily |
| Closed: | for lunch & Sunday |

### How To Get There
Take the A16 from Calais to Boulogne. exit for the N42 signs to St. Omer and St. Martin-B. Follow the N42 through the town on the Route de St Omer.
Turn left into Rue de la Colonne and then take third right into rue Pasteur.

This outlet specialises in the wines of just one region of France - the Languedoc. Here you can discover the delights of this southern area of France in bottles or on draught (en vrac).

If you choose to buy these sun-fortified wines en vrac, you can carry them away in 10 or 20 litre cubis. Make sure you decant these within six weeks.

Probably their best tipple is the **Muscat de Riversaltes AOC**, a wine for which the Languedoc area is famous. It is a sweet dessert wine, but do as the French do and serve it chilled and enjoy as an aperitif.

A reasonable but simple red **Vin du Pays d L'Aude** is available at £1.10 a litre and for a little more (£1.80 a litre) you can buy a Corbieres AOC.

# Mille Vignes Wine Merchant

## Mille Vignes

90 Rue Carnot, 62930
Wimereux

Tel: 00 33 (0)3 21 32 60 13

| | |
|---|---|
| Map Ref: | follow A6 |
| Bus No: | - |
| English: | Yes |
| Tasting: | Yes |
| Payment: | [cards] |
| Parking: | Opposite the shop and off street |
| Open: | Tuesday - Saturday 10.00-13.30 and 14.30-19.00. Sunday 10.00-13.00 |
| Closed: | Monday |

The owner of Mille Vignes is an Englishman with a palate, it seems, for fine French wine. It was this passion that led to this wine outlet in France selling quality French wines.

Mille Vignes, a cosy, corner outlet, was opened by the Mayor of Wimereux. The owner, a silversmith by trade leaves the management of Mille Vignes to Nick Sweet - another Englishman and connoisseur of wines with a long history in wine.

### How To Get There

From Calais port take the A6/A26 motorway towards Dunkerque and then Boulogne. Turn off at Junction 4 signed posted Wimilles/Wimereux Nord. Follow signs for centre of Wimereux.

## BEST FRENCH WINE MERCHANT IN BOULOGNE

Nick has chosen the selection and is happy to guide you. The speciality is wines from the Rhône, Loire, white Burgundy, Claret from family-owned domaines and châteaux. Amid their consistently good selection there are many wines to recommend

### ★ STAR BUYS ★

**Domaine de Montpezat Sauvignon Vin de Pays d'Oc 2000 £2.90**
Terrific Sauvignon aromas and a good zesty palate. Highly successful example, well priced.

# Mille Vignes Wine Merchant

Pico Domaine du Poujol
Vin de Pays de L'Herault
2000 £3.30
Attractive, characterful dry
white, nicely scented and
very crisp.

Château Etang des
Colombes Bicentaire
Vieilles Vignes 1998 £4.50
Dry and quite restrained,
with spicy, peppery
undertones. Somewhat
exotic in style, finishes a
touch short. Needs a year
or two, best with food.

Rasteau Côtes du Rhône
Villages Domaine St Gayan
1998 £4.50
Fine, sweet, dried fruit
aromas and a gloriously
rich palate which
epitomises the great quality
of the 1998 vintage.
Already drinking very well.

Gigondas Domaine Font-
Sane 1998 £7.50
Really top class Rhône red,
again showing the
excellence of the vintage
but with an added
dimension which will benefit
from further ageing. Dry,
flavoursome and very long.

# Le Touquet

*There is only one word for*

*Le Touquet*

*....Style*

You know you have entered Le Touquet when the road ahead changes colour as if laid out like a regal red carpet. It may seem a little pretentious but this is just the beginning of your journey into style.

Shoppers can relish the chic designer shops while sun worshippers can enjoy the fabulously clean and well maintained seafront and beach - either below the promenade or more discretely in the dunes.

The sporty sort can sail, windsurf or even take instruction in sand yachting from none other than Bertrand Lambert - the world champion.

Equestrian enthusiasts should head for the shady beauty of the forest and indulge in horse jumping or racing at the Hippodrome It is located within the grounds of the Parc International de la Canche where a well established equestrian school is run. The centre also arranges romantic horse rides along the coast at dawn, and sometimes, when the night is clear, even in moonlight.

Tennis players can play on the same outdoor or on indoor courts (with natural light) where champions have played before.

Le Touquet has its own golf course which has the double accolade

# Le Touquet

of being the international championship course and considered the most beautiful in France. Tee-off at either of their two 18-hole courses in France.

Located on the seafront is a Thallasa health and relaxation centre where clients are pampered with concoctions containing oceanic minerals. their health 'cures' are designed to rejuvenate, stimulate, invigorate or relax.

Meanwhile the kids can enjoy a day at the Aqualud water adventure park also on the seafront - a fabulous tropical themed indoor and outdoor swimming pool with flumes, water toboggans and other pool side rides.

Culture vultures need only stroll through the pristine streets and

observe as the diverse architectural history unfolds. The buildings are a collage of several varieties of seaside styles from different eras.

Although they are startlingly different from each other, they somehow blend well together. The differing styles have evolved because, amazingly, while Le Touquet's neighbouring coastal towns were destroyed by the wars, Le Touquet itself remained unscathed. Moreover, it was during the period

**How to get to Le Touquet**
From Calais take the A16 motorway in the direction of Dunkerque. Follow motorway signs to Boulogne. Between Boulogne and Le Touquet there is a toll to pay. Exit at Junction (sortie 26) at Etaple, Le Touquet. Simply follow the signs.

between the two world wars that Le Touquet rose to the stature of chic in the eyes of British holidaymakers.

**The Past**

The history of the town started in the hands of a notary called Alphonse Daloz.  He bought the land in1837 in the hope that it was arable.  He planted an assortment of vegetables and cereals, pine and other attractive trees.  Only the trees survived, but when these matured by the end of the century Le Touquet had become a most appealing forest by the sea.  The director of Le Figaro newspaper was so inspired by Le Touquet's beauty that he considered it an ideal holiday resort.

Le Touquet's prosperity was sealed when In 1903 two  Englishman, John Whitely and Allen Stoneham bought the forest (known then as la Fôret) and formed a company called Le Touquet Syndicat Ltd. The company  built expensive villas and hotels and sold the villas  to the rich and famous of London.  The extensive advertising in the British media contributed much to the general awareness of Le Touquet.

Soon famous names such as P.G. Wodehouse and Noel Coward bought villas within the forest and the luxury hotels filled up with weekending English nobility.

By the 1920's it had become **the** place for the jet set to weekend.These days it is mostly the rich Parisiens who own the expensive villas in the forest. Some say it is like a little bit of Paris by the sea and this belief is reflected in the name Le Touquet Paris-Plage.

# Le Touquet

**Tourist Office**
Palais de l'Europe
Place de l'Hermitage
Le Touquet
Tel 00 33 (0)3 21 06 72 00

**Covered Market**
rue Jean Monnet
Open daily from April

**Race Course**
Ave de la Dune aux Loups
Tel: 00 33 (0)321 05 15 25

**Pony Rides**
Hippodrome de la Canche
Tel: 00 33 (0)3 21 05 20 97

**Sailing activities:**

**Base Nautique Nord**
Cercle Nautique du Touquet
Tel: 00 33 (0)3 21 05 12 77

Bas Nautique Sud:

**Speed-sailing**
Hervé Spriet
Tel: 00 33 (0)1 42 88 09 43

**Sand Yachting**
Bertrand Lambert
Tel: 00 33 (0)3 21 05 33 51

**Golf du Touquet**
Avenue du Golf - BP41
Tel: 00 33 (0)3 21 06 28 00
Two 18-hole golf courses

**Swimming**
Aqualud - Parc Aquatic
Tel: 00 33 (0)3 21 05 63 59

**Thalassotherapy**
Sea front
Tel: 00 33 (0)3 21 09 86 00

**Le Touquet Museum**
Corner of Avenue du Golf
and Avenue du Château
Tel 00 33 (0)3 21 05 62 62

**Tennis** Club des 4 Saisons
Avenue de l'Hippodrome
Open daily 08.00-22.00rhrs
Tel: 00 33 (0)3 21 05 02 97

---

### A Must See - Life at Sea

Just before Le Touquet you
will pass through a fishing
village called Étaples Sur
Mer. Stop off here and visit
the **Maréis Museum.** This
new museum depicts the life
of the local fishermen and
their wives. There are several
displays - some interactive,
3D films and a touch pool.

**Maréis Museum**
Centre de la Pêche
Artisanale, La Corderie
Boulevard Bigot-Descelers
62630 Etaples Sur Mer
Tel: 00 33 (0)321 09 04 00
www.pas-de-calais.com
Adults £4.50 Kids £3

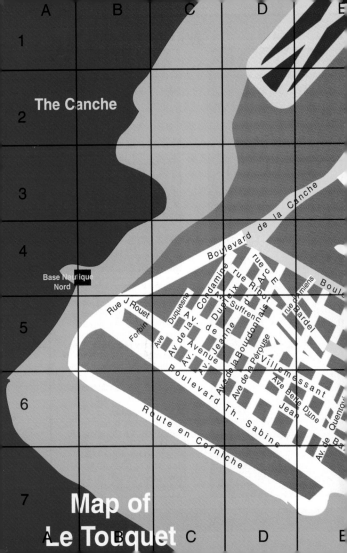

Map of
Le Touquet

The Canche

Base Nautique
Nord

Boulevard de la Canche

Rue J. Rouet

Forbin

Ave

Av. de la

Avenue

Av.

Duquesne

Coldampre

Av. de Jeanne

rue Ribot

rue E. Arch

Duclaix

Suffrennais

rue Pardel

rue Amiens

Boul

Av. de la Bourdonne

Ave de la Pérouse

Villemessant

Boulevard

Th. Sabine

Ave Belle Dune

Jean

Av. de Ba

Quentovi

Route en Corniche

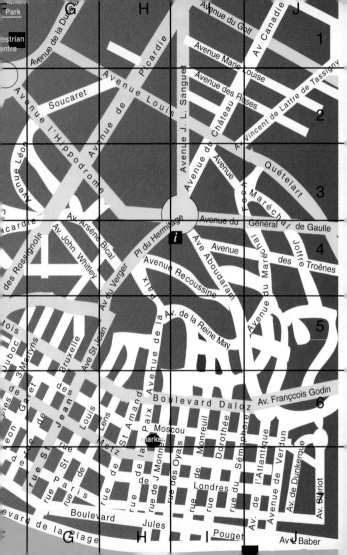

## *A Tour Around The Shops -*
## *Most of which are*
## *branches of Paris shops*

The best shopping is at **Rue St Jean**. The road stretches from the seafront to the Casino and the fabulous Westminster Hotel.

Our tour starts at the seafront.

### 5 Nota Bene Pia
This shop specialises in stylish Aigle shoe wear. No self- respecting local would be seen on the beach promenade in anything less. It's a jet set thing.

### 7 Geko
Sells ethnic style products and jewellery including cowboy hats made of real cow hide. How chic!

### 9 Flais Gérard
Antique lovers would be impressed with this shop. It exudes style. Even before you enter, the extensive wood carvings decorating the exterior top to bottom create quite an impression. Inside there is a mixture of French and other European antiquities that any antique officianado would be proud to display.

### 12 Comptoir des Isles
This shop must be for the gentry. On the shelves is a strange mix of products such as quality bric-à-brac and some lovely - if a little frumpish - clothes.

### 14 Betty Bop
A complete contrast to number 12. All the clothes here are full of pretty, girly, flouncey frills

## 6 Carat
An expensive jewellery shop but the designs are quite stunning.

## 21 Barque en Ciel
This is a play on the words "arc-en-ciel' - a rainbow. It is a lovely seaside shop selling sea shells and maritime toys. There are also some fantastic ships complete with sails, available in many sizes including miniatures.

## 33 Love Love
A bedtime shop for, it would seem, eccentric bachelors. Socks come with corny cartoon pictures to match boxer shorts and slippers. A set with teddy bears is particularly lovely.

## 35. Paris Voy
This is a lingerie shop for the modest woman however, there are some sexy stockings on display in the window.

## 36 Only Cool People
If you think your children are trendy, this is the place to shop for them.

## 37 Rien Que Pour Elles/Lui
Whoever your favourite designer is you are bound to find something of their collection at this chic outlet. Labels include Paul Smith, Moschino and Jean Paul Gaultier.

## 38 Les P'tits Branchés
More stylish clothes for but for slightly older trendy teens.

## 40 Chez Martin
Looking good on the golf course or the tennis courts is essential for serious players. Chez Martine are specialists in providing the winning kit.

## 42 Rodier
Rodier offer beautiful and stylish clothes for women.

# Le Touquet Shops

### 43 Les Poteries du Logis
This quaint shop sells pretty pottery with a rustic feel.

### 7 Au Chat Bleu
Chocoholics will love Le Chat Bleu. It is famous throughout Le Touquet for its divine hand-made chocolates. The owners insist that they invented 'Le Bouchée' - literally a mouthful but actually a chocolate bar. Choose from 56 varieties.

### 48 Terrne et Ciel d'Opale
A quality gift shop selling dolls, books, trinkets and divinely scented soaps.

### 56-61 La Mascotte
La Mascotte is a series of shops located on both sides of rue St Jean. It is somewhat of shopping centre for an endless range of quality goods. It is the shop the jet set place their wedding lists. British tourists in the know come here to get their hands on Lalique crystal at one third off the UK price. Everyone shops here for their leather bags, Cartier, Hermès, Baccarat and Christofle products. All in all this is a lovely place to browse.

### 89 Florence Kooijman
This small shop is named after its owner Florence Kooijman. The enterprising  young shoe designer, Florence, designs all the shoes on display. She has also developed an interesting concept in shoe buying: If you like a shoe but not the colour or even the material, choose from a range of swatches and the shoes will be made to order within two weeks.

**Special offer:**
Show your guide and get **10% discount** on your purchases at Florence Kooijman.

# Le Touquet Sights

## *The town of Le Touquet is in itself a "Sight". Just walk around*

Nestling between the sea and the forest Le Touquet offers a range of sights. As the resort developed, different architects left their mark making the streets an exhibition of diverse architecture.

The area of **Le Village Suisse**, for instance, is tinged with medieval influences, whereas Villa le Castel in **rue Jean Monnet** shows off its neo-medieval style. **Avenue de la Reine Victoria** on the other hand has two adjoining buildings Villa Glenwood and Villa Karidja built with exceptional style in symmetry.

As in any French town Le Touquet's Town Hall in **rue des Oyats** represents a lovely architectural feature. It is made from local stone and flanked by an imposing belfry. Its chunky features are very 1920s Anglo-Norman, resembling a lord's manor house.

To learn more about the endless architectural styles, visit Le Touquet Museum on **Avenue du Golf** for a good review of the architectural history. The museum itself is housed in a typically handsome 1930s Le Touquettois villa. Paintings by the noted landscape artist **Edouard Leveque** are on display within the museum. It was through his paintings that Leveque inadvertently gave the Opal Coast its name. His palette consisted mainly of pinks, beiges and slightly iridescent colours resembling the hues of opal stone.

**Rue St Jean** is probably the liveliest area especially

around the beach, where you can walk on the promenade, bathe in the sun shine or the sea, or participate in beach sports.

On the sea front look out for the diving board. It may seem odd to include a diving board in a town's list of monumental heritage, but this is no ordinary diving board - it was the first diving board to appear in France. When built in 1948 by the architect Louis Quételard it was very futuristic structure and became synonymous with "le Style Touquettois Moderne". Anyone bold enough to use the board was regarded as fashionably avant garde - and if that someone was a women in a bathing suit even a tad risqué. Today it remains a symbol of modernity of post-war Le Touquet

**Rue Jeanne Monnet** leads to the arch of the covered market. Unlike other markets this moon-shaped monument, decorated with off white tiles is a listed building. The beautiful, brick built, white-washed structure was the design of the architect Henry-Léon Bloch and built between 1927-1937. The market's covered area, adorned with attractive tiling, is where the perishable products such as cheese, meat, fish, fruit and vegetables are sold. The central courtyard is covered with stalls selling superb top quality textiles, clothes and shoes at market prices.

Apart from the colourful echoes of French life the market also offers two fine vistas: the sea and the Jardin d'Ypres.

The 1900 acre forest is very well-manicured. The trees include maritime pine, birch, alder, poplar and acacia which offer shelter from the wind for around 2000 Anglo-Norman and modern luxury villas.

# A Detour to Montreuil Sur Mer

*As you walk over cobbled stones and medieval streets, you feel you have walked back in time to a bygone age*

Just a short drive from Le Touquet is the delightful town of Montreuil Sur Mer. The area, located on the edge of a plateau, overlooks the Canche Valley. It was once connected to the sea by an estuary channel. Though the sea has receded, the name was retained.

The ancient town unfolds over the slope of a tall hill, crowned at its apex by the remains of a medieval castle.

The streets, especially in the centre, are delightfully cobbled. Every now and again here are tiny alleyways, no wider than a doorway, winding themselves through the town and acting as short cuts to other streets. The oldest street in the town is Rue Clapen-bas, noted for its tiny buildings.

Probably the most impressive historical remains are the ramparts. The fortress was initially built in the 9th century by Count Helgauld II, and later reinforced in the 10th century. It was partly demolished in the 16th century after the siege of1537 which led to the abandonment of the lower city wall. Its remains are noted as one of the oldest preserved urban stone walls in France.

It seems quite fitting that with such a medieval feel all around Montreuil sur Mer should be a town that specialises in antiques. Every year the town turns intself into an outdoor antiques market. More than 420 stalls set up selling a myriad of antique to eager buyers from around France and Europe.

There is also a public antique auction held every weekend. The auction, run by the flamboyant Henri Anton, is held in a huge warehouse (20 rue Pierre Ledent tel: 00 33 (0)3 21 06 05 70) filled with a dazzling array of antique bric-à-brac, wine, toys, furniture and artefacts. Entry is from 10am but auctioning starts at 2.30pm.

Victor Hugo, the famous 19th century novelist and writer, spent a brief time in Montreuil. During his stay he became inspired to write **Les Misérables**. The novel recalls the years of the Napoleonic Empire and the 1830 revolution. Every year the story is turned into an outdoor spectacle of music and light which anyone can attend.

How to Get to Montreuil
Take the N1 from Calais
or N39 from Le Touquet

## Highlights

**Les Miserables**
**The Citadelle**
**July and August**
The whole of the grounds of the citadel is turned into an outdoor theatre. Many townsfolk act out the play Les Misérables written by Victor Hugo in Montreuil Sur Mer. The impressively grand and colourful spectacle is complemented with lights and music. Though it is in French, the sequence of scenes and music can be interpreted in any language. Contact the tourist office for information.

**Spring Antique Market**
**14th -16th April**
420 exhibitors set up in the town centre forming an outdoor antiques market. More information is available from the tourist office.

**Saturday Market**
Place de General de Gaulle

**Montreuil Tourist Office**
**21 rue Carnot**
62170 Montreuil-Sur Mer
Tel: 00 33 (0)321 06 04 27

# That's The Spirit - The Tipple Table

100 of the most popular products in alphabetical order. Where possible we have included the average UK price so that you can see your savings at a glance. Prices have been converted to sterling. Prices tend to fluctuate, usually within a 5% band.

## TIPPLE TABLE - PRICES ARE IN £ STERLING

| PPRODUCT | % vol | Ave UK price | Auchan | Carrefour | Sainsbury | Tesco |
|---|---|---|---|---|---|---|
| Aberlour Scotch Whisky 10yrs 70cl | 43 | 19.99 | 11.62 | 12.09 | 13.99 | 12.70 |
| Absolut Vodka 70cl | 40 | 13.09 | 8.55 | | 11.10 | 13.70 |
| Bacardi White Rum 1L | 37.5 | 14.99 | 10.30 | 10.30 | 11.49 | 10.00 |
| Baileys Irish Cream 70cl | 17 | 16.95 | 7.65 | 7.36 | 10.95 | 10.50 |
| Ballantines 70cl | 40 | | 8.20 | 8.70 | | |
| Beefeater London Dry Gin 70cl | 40 | 12.44 | 8.28 | | | 9.80 |
| Bells *70cl 1L | 40 | 16.49 | 8.81* | | 12.49 | 11.50 |
| Benedictine 70cl | 40 | 16.99 | 10.68 | 10.61 | | |
| Black & White Scotch Whisky 70cl | 40 | | 6.88 | 7.36 | | |
| Bombay Sapphire London Dry Gin 70cl | 40 | 12.99 | 10.70 | | | 9.50 |
| Calvados 70cl | 40 | | | 8.44 | | |
| Campari 1L | 25 | 16.15 | 8.90 | 9.06 | 8.99 | 8.66 |
| Canadian Club Whisky 70c | 40 | 14.99 | 7.13 | 7.61 | 9.99 | 9.69 |
| Canadian Mist Whisky 70cl | 40 | | 6.80 | | | 7.12 |
| Captain Morgan 1L | 40 | 16.99 | | | | 10.59 |
| Cardhu Single Malt 70cl | 40 | 17.22 | 18.00 | | | |
| Chivas Regal Scotch Whisky 12 yrs 70cl | 40 | 19.99 | 14.87 | 14.88 | 15.95 | 14.90 |
| Cinzano Bianco 1L *75cl | 16 | *4.99 | 4.07 | | | 3.90 |
| Cinzano Rosso 1L | 16 | | 3.87 | 3.90 | | |
| Clan Campbell 70cl | 40 | | 7.21 | 7.52 | | |
| Clès Des Ducs Armagnac 70cl | 40 | | 8.72 | 8.67 | | 11.22 |
| Cointreau 70cl | 40 | 16.18 | 9.30 | 10.07 | 9.05 | 9.10 |
| Courvoisier Cognac 70cl | 40 | 20.34 | 14.60 | | | 13.20 |
| Croft Tawny Port 75cl | 19.5 | | 5.40 | | | |
| Cutty Sark Scotch Whisky 70cl | 40 | | 8.00 | 8.37 | | |
| Dimple 70cl | 40 | | 17.57 | 15.93 | | |
| Drambuie 70cl | 40 | 14.99 | 18.88 | | 11.49 | 15.80 |
| Dubonnet 1L | 16 | 7.48 | 4.54 | 4.88 | | |

# That's The Spirit - The Tipple Table

| PRODUCT | % vol | Ave UK price | Auchan | Carrefour | Sainsbury | Tesco |
|---|---|---|---|---|---|---|
| Famous Grouse Scotch Whisky 70cl *1L | 40 | 16.99 | 8.85 | 9.30 | 12.99* | 8.91 |
| Four Roses Bourbon Scotch Whisky 70cl | 40 | | 8.24 | 8.55 | | |
| Gilbey's London Dry Gin 70cl | 37.5 | | 6.00 | 6.33 | | |
| Glen Rogers Scotch Whisky 8yrs 70cl | 40 | | 8.86 | 8.88 | | |
| Glen Turner Pure Malt 8yrs 70cl | 40 | | 9.18 | 9.26 | | |
| Glenfiddich 70cl | 40 | 21.10 | 12.72 | 13.00 | | 13.00 |
| Glenlivet 12 yrs 70cl | 40 | 19.99 | 15.78 | 15.78 | | 14.80 |
| Glenmorangie 10yrs 70cl | 40 | 22.99 | 17.20 | 17.71 | 17.99 | 15.80 |
| Gold River 8yrs 70cl | 30 | | | 6.43 | | |
| Gordon's London Dry Gin 1L | 37.5 | 15.48 | 9.98 | 10.10 | 10.99 | 11.00 |
| Grand Marnier Liqueur 70cl | 40 | 14.29 | 10.44 | 11.07 | 10.29 | 15.80 |
| Grants Whisky 70cl | 40 | 15.39 | 7.00 | 7.00 | 9.99 | 7.10 |
| Haig Gold Label 70cl | 40 | | 6.94 | | | |
| Harveys Bristol Cream 1L | 17.5 | 7.89 | | | | 6.70 |
| Hennessy Cognac 1L *70cl | 40 | | 14.82 | 20.44 | | |
| J&B Whisky 70cl | 40 | 14.99 | 8.72 | | 11.99 | 11.90 |
| Jack Daniels Whisky 70cl | 43 | 17.29 | 10.95 | 11.48 | 11.90 | 14.50 |
| Jameson Irish Whiskey 70cl | 40 | 13.99 | 8.78 | | 10.99 | 9.27 |
| Janneau Grand Armagnac 1L * 70cl | 40 | *9.44 | 12.24 | | | |
| Jim Bean Bourbon 70cl | 40 | 14.44 | 9.20 | 9.46 | 10.99 | 9.50 |
| Johnnie Walker Black Label 70cl | 40 | 16.49 | 11.92 | | 14.95 | 14.50 |
| Johnnie Walker Red Label 1L | 40 | 16.90 | 8.24 | 10.98 | 14.94 | |
| Kahlua Liqueur 70cl | 26 | 12.99 | 9.62 | | 9.59 | 8.00 |
| Knockando Whisky 70cl | 43 | 19.99 | 19.90 | | 14.99 | |
| Label 5 70cl | 40 | | 6.79 | 7.15 | | |
| Lambs Navy Rum 70cl | 40 | 11.95 | | | 8.95 | 8.50 |
| Laphroaig 70cl | 43 | 22.99 | | | 18.99 | 16.60 |
| Laphroaig 10 yrs 70cl | 40 | | 17.78 | | | |
| Long John Scotch Whisky 70cl | 40 | | 6.69 | 7.13 | | |
| Macallan 70cl | 43 | 22.99 | | 21.17 | 17.49 | 16.00 |
| MacArthur's 70cl | 40 | | 9.99 | | | |
| Malibu white rum 1L 70cl | 21 | 15.49 | 8.50 | *6.22 | 9.49 | 9.50 |

| PRODUCT | % vol | Ave UK price | Auchan | Carrefour | Sainsbury | Tesco |
|---|---|---|---|---|---|---|
| Martell 3 Star Cognac 70cl | 40 | 25.49 | 12.74 | 13.45 | | 12.50 |
| Martini Bianco 1L | 16 | 5.99 | 4.92 | 4.90 | | 4.97 |
| Martini Rosé 1L | 16 | 5.99 | 5.48 | 5.40 | | 4.94 |
| Martini Rosso 1L | 16 | 5.99 | 4.70 | 4.82 | | 4.94 |
| Negrita Rum 1L | 40 | | 5.15 | 7.10 | | |
| Noilly Prat 1L *75cl | 18 | *5.99 | 5.56 | 5.55 | | 5.54 |
| Old Lady's London Dry Gin 70cl | 37.5 | | 6.75 | 5.66 | | |
| Old Virginia Bourbon 70cl | 40 | | 7.64 | 7.65 | | |
| Pastis 51 1L | 45 | | 6.64 | 7.30 | | |
| Pernod 1L *75cl | 15 | 13.99 | 10.59 | 10.52 | 9.99 | 11.55 |
| Pimms 70cl | 25 | 15.99 | 7.60 | 7.18 | 9.99 | 10.49 |
| Remy Martin VSOP 70cl | 40 | 26.18 | 17.73 | 18.64 | | 17.40 |
| Ricard Pastis 70cl | 45 | | 9.87 | 10.50 | | |
| Sandeman Port 75cl | 19 | | 6.00 | 5.50 | | |
| Smirnoff Vodka 70cl | 37.5 | 13.99 | 7.85 | 7.05 | 10.99 | 10.80 |
| St James White Rum 70CL | 40 | | 7.33 | 6.80 | | |
| Southern Comfort 70cl | 40 | 14.99 | 10.17 | 10.12 | | 11.00 |
| Stones Original Ginger Wine 70cl | n/a | 5.19 | | | | 4.69 |
| Teachers Scotch Whisky 70cl | 40 | 11.69 | 8.83 | 7.90 | | 8.87 |
| Tia Maria 70cl *50 | 26.5 | 18.99 | *6.90 | 9.35 | 12.99 | 12.61 |
| Vladivar Vodka 1L | 37.5 | 13.64 | | | | 8.64 |
| Warninks Advocaat 70cl | 17.2 | 9.99 | | | | 7.66 |
| White Horse Scotch Whisky 70cl | 40 | 10.99 | | | | 8.37 |
| Whyte & Mackay Special Reserve 70cl | 40 | 11.29 | 7.34 | 7.36 | | |
| Wild Turkey No.8 Bourbon Whisky 70cl | 43.4 | | 9.00 | 9.56 | | |
| William Lawson Scotch Whisky 70cl *1L | 40 | | 7.95 | 7.51 | | |
| William Peel 70cl *1L | 40 | | *11.90 | 6.78 | | |
| Wyborowa Vodka 70cl | 40 | | 7.54 | | | |
| Zubrowka Vodka 70cl | 40 | | 9.02 | 85.65 | | |

# Which Wine?

France is one of the leading wine producing countries and this is reflected in the French outlets where most, if not all, of their selection is French. With so much choice, it helps to know a little about French wine.

First, inspect the label for an indication and therefore an assurance of the quality of the wine. The best wines of the regions have Appéllation Contrôlées on the label which gives a guarantee of the origin, supervision of production method, variety of grape and quantity produced.

Less controlled but still good value wines are listed as Vins Délimités de Qualité Supérieure (VDQS) and are worth trying. There are also the Vins de Pays. These are country wines, more widely found in the South of France, which do not specify the exact location of the vineyard but are generally worth a try and often offer the best value for money. Good

examples are Vin de Pays du Gard and the wines from Côtes de Gascogne. Further down the ladder are the Vins de Table. They are varied in quality but are so cheap that they are worth a gamble. You could be surprised for as little at 55p-£1.33.

We have categorised the wine growing areas broadly into seven major regions. These are: Alsace, Burgundy, Bordeaux, Champagne, Loire, Midi and Rhône.

# Which Wine?

## Alsace

The Alsace is situated in eastern France on the German border.

The wine labels from this area differ from the rest of France by calling the wine by the name of the grape rather than the area e.g. Gewürztraminer, Riesling.

If a label reads Alsace AC, this is the standard Alsace wine which is typically Germanic in character, often being aromatic and fruity, but drier than its German equivalent.

A label with Alsace Grand Cru printed on it indicates a higher quality and only the four most highly regarded grape types can be used in its making and they are: Gewürztraminer, Riesling (not to be confused with the German wine of the same name), Tokay Pinot and Muscat. These are medium priced white wines with reliable quality and are generally dry to medium dry. The Alsatian wines are great aperitifs and also combine well with fish, poultry, salads or with a summer meal.

Expect to pay: £1.66-£3.33 per bottle.

## Bordeaux

Bordeaux is in the southwest region of France with the Dordogne region on its eastern border and the Atlantic Ocean on the west.

The term Claret refers to the red dry wines of this region and wines such as Médoc, St. Emillion and Pomerol which are in the lower price range.

There are also numerous wines known by the name of Château. Quality, especially at the lower end, can be variable. Claret goes well with meat, chicken and cheese.

Expect to pay: From as little as £1.55 per bottle, to more than £12.50 for a top class Château.

## Which Wine?

Situated between Bordeaux and the Dordogne valley is an area called Bergerac.

Bergerac has a complete range of wines of its own; most commonly Bergerac (red, rosé and dry white), Côtes de Bergerac (red and medium sweet wine), Monbazillac (sweet white) and Pécharmant (fine red).

Expect to pay: £1.10-£1.77 for the Bergerac. £3.33 for Monbazillac.

Burgundy
Burgundy is an area of France southeast of Paris running from Chablis at the northern end, down through to Lyon at the southern end. About 75% of the wine production in this region is red with the remainder white.

It is worth noting the area on the label when choosing a Burgundy wine since the more exact the area, the finer the wine is likely to be. The best are labelled "Grand Cru",followed by

"Premier Cru", "Villages", a specified region and finally, the most basic will have just Burgundy. The best known of the whites is Chablis which is in the higher price bracket. The Côte de Beaune produces some of the finest such as Meursault and some good light dry wines come from Mâconnais such as Mâcon Blanc and Pouilly Fuissé. All Burgundy white wines are dry and are an ideal accompaniment for fish.

The finest red Burgundy wine comes from the Côtes de Nuits such as Nuits St Georges and the Côtes de Beaune namely Pommard, Volnay and Monthélie. These are best drunk with meat, game and cheese.

Expect to pay: £3.80-£7.80 These wines tend to be reliable in this price point.

Best known of the reds in the south of this region is Beaujolais. This is divided into the standard Beaujolais AC, Beaujolais

# Which Wine?

Supérieur which denotes a slightly higher alcohol content and Beaujolais-Villages - an appéllation controllée (quality control) given to about 40 villages and considered to be of superior quality.

The most prestigious of these wines bear the name of one of the 10 communes (crus). They are worth noting since you will come across them practically everywhere. They are Saint-Amour, Juliénas, Chénas, Moulin-à-Vent, Fleurie, Chiroubles, Morgon, Brouilly, Côte de Brouilly and Régnié (the most recently created, but least distinguished cru). These are medium priced red dry fruity wines with the villages and communes especially reliable and should be drunk young and served slightly chilled.

Expect to pay: £1.11-£2.80 for basic Beaujolais AC. £1.90-£5.70 per bottle for Beaujolais- Villages or named Commune.

Midi
(Languedoc Roussillon and Provence)
This region stretches from northeast of Marseilles down to the west of Perpignan bordering Spain. Wines from this region, such as Minervois and Corbières, represent good value dry reds. The Vin de Pays (sometimes referred to as country wines) of the area offer the best value of all. The label shows the Vin de Pays description followed by the region.

Expect to pay: 60p-£2.30 per bottle and a little more if VDQS (Vins Délimités de Qualité Supérieure) is printed on the label.

Rhône
This area is located south of the Burgundy region and continues due south to the Mediterranean near Marseilles. The region generally produces robust, full bodied wines. There is a standard Côtes du Rhône and a Côtes du Rhône Villages, famous for its dry

# Which Wine?

red wine. If the wine is attributable to a named village (shown on the label) the chances are it will be better quality but more expensive. Côtes du Rhône wines accompany cheese and poultry dishes very well.

Expect to pay: 88p-£2.22 for Côtes du Rhône label wines. £2.22-£3.33 for Côtes du Rhône Villages.

## Loire

The Loire wine region starts at Nantes on the western Atlantic coast of France and follows the Loire River east to Orléans where it cuts back southeast to Sancerre. The majority of wines produced in this area are white. The Loire offers a wide variety of wine and all have a certain refreshing quality that comes from its northerly position the character of the soil.

Among the many well known names from this area are Muscadet, Gros Plant Du Nantais, Pouilly-Fumé and Sancerre all dry whites, and Anjou which is well known for its Rosé. The versatile Rosé can be drunk throughout the meal. The whites are best with fish and salads.

# Which Wine?

Although named wines are generally a better buy, in our experience it is especially true for Muscadet where we recommend either a named or "sur lie".

Expect to pay: 88p-£1.66 for Gros Plant. £1.11-£2.44 for Muscadet. £3.88-£4.33) for Sancerre & Pouilly Fumé £1.11-£1.77 for Anjou Rosé wines.

If you prefer a medium dry wine then try the Vouvray at £2.50-£3.50. It is also available as sparkling wine.

Champagne
*"I am drinking stars"*
Dom Perignon describing his sparkling wine

The most luxurious drink in the world, sparkling wine, suggests celebration - something special. Situated northeast of Paris with Reims and Epernay at the heart, Champagne is renowned for its sparkling wine. The climate, the soil, the art of the wine maker and, of course, the grapes all combine to make champagne the most celebrated in terms of

unmatched quality and reputation. These are usually sold under a brand name e.g. Bollinger, Moët et Chandon, Mumm, Veuve Clicquot etc which are nearly always dry. If you do not like dry wines, then ask for a demi-sec or even a rosé champagne. Only wine made in the champagne area is entitled to be called Champagne. Other wines of this type is referred to as "sparkling" wine. Some have Méthode Traditionnelle on the label which means made in the "Champagne method".

Expect to pay: £5.90-£7.77 for lesser known brands. £12.00 upwards for well-known brands.

| Champagne comes in the following sizes | |
|---|---|
| Quart: | 20cl |
| Half-bottle: | 37.5cl |
| Bottle: | 75cl |
| Magnum: | 2 bottles |
| Jeroboam: | 4 bottles |
| Mathusalah: | 8 bottles |
| Salmanazar | 12 bottles |
| Balthazar: | 16 bottles |
| Nebuchadnezzar: | 20 bottles |

# Champagne Charlies?

*"Remember gentleman, it's not just France we are fighting for, it's champagne!"*
**Winston S Churchill, 1918**

Never has so much been said by so many about just one style of wine. It seems everyone loves to drink champagne and that includes the Brits. But why are we being charged so much more than the French for the pleasure?

The reason, it seems, is simply because they can. But who are "they"? Perhaps "they" are the champagne houses, who seem to have a unique pricing policy for each country. Are they charging our retailers higher prices who in turn are inevitably forced to pass on the cost?

Or perhaps "they" are the retailers cashing in on an opportunity to make a profit. One source claims the difference is exchange-rate driven. It's a grey area and no one is rushing to make it black and white.

Nevertheless, while the status quo remains, you can save on average £6.50 a bottle. If you were to buy to the 75 bottles limit of bubbly allowed by Customs & Excise for a wedding or celebration you will have made a massive saving of £487.50! Now that is something to celebrate.

| Champagne | Av.UK | Av.France |
|---|---|---|
| Canard Duchêne | £15.50 | £10.90 |
| Lanson Black Label | £20.99 | £12.50 |
| Laurent Perrier | £21.00 | £14.00 |
| Mercier Brut | £17.00 | £12.50 |
| Moët et Chandon | £20.99 | £16.00 |
| Mumm Cordon Rouge | £19.49 | £15.50 |
| Nicolas Feuillate | £16.99 | £9.50 |
| Piper Heidsieck | £18.99 | £13.00 |
| Veuve Clicquot Ponsardin | £23.00 | £16.20 |

# Here For The Beer?

*Without a doubt, the best bargain to be had in France is the beer. With savings of up to 50 per cent beer drinkers are certainly not bitter !*

Fortunately, beer is in abundance in Calais and Boulogne and the most widely available beers tend to be continental. The average continental beer has an alcoholic content of at least 4.5% which is more than 1% stronger than the average British bitter.

You may find 'promos' offering beers cheaply but these could be lower alcohol beers such as Kœnigsbier or Brandeberg. These retail at around £2.80 for 24 bottles but have an alcoholic volume of only 2.80%.

The majority of continental beers are light in colour and are best served chilled. They are sold in 25cl bottles which equates to just under half a pint (0.43).

The highest alcoholic beers tend to be from Belgium. The more popular ones include Hoegaarden (5% ABV) known as Witbier or

Bière Blanche meaning white beer and refers to its naturally cloudy appearance. Although in Britain cloudiness is usually associated with the beer being past its best, in this case it is due to its production process and ingredients: barley, unmalted wheat, Styrian and Kent hops, coriander and çuraçao. As it brews, the top-fermenting yeast turns the malt to alcohol, but because the wheat is not malted, the starches contribute to the final cloudy appearance.

Possibly the best known Belgian beers are Trappist beers made by monks in just 5 monasteries in Belgium. These include Chimay Red (7%) - copper colour and slightly sweet, Chimay White (6.3%) - lots of hop and slightly acidic, Chimay Blue (7.1%) - fruity aromas, Orval (6.2%) - orange hue, with acidity; Rochefort 6,8,10 (ABVs are 7.3%, 7.5% and 11.3%) - characteristics range from russet colour with a herbal palate, tawny and fruity to dark brown with chocolate and fruity palate respectively.

Pilsner-style beers include the mass marketed beers of Jupiler, a dry and soft easy drinking example and Stella Artois (the biggest brewing company in Belgium) who also make Leffe - an abbey style ale.

France itself has two brewing regions. The first is in the north around the city of Lille, the most well known part being French Flanders. The style of beer produced - bière de garde - resembles its Belgian counterparts. Strasbourg, in the east is the other brewing region. The final product is similar to German lagers.

The major French breweries are Kronenbourg/Kanterbrau, Mutzig and Pelforth. The latter is situated near Lille and owned by Heineken, and produces light and dark lagers: Pelforth Blonde (5.8% ) and Pelforth Brune (5.2% & 6.5%).

There are also popular beers from Australia such as Castlemain XXXX and the sweetish Fosters lager (both 4%) which are widely available.

Products from many British breweries also share shelf space in northern France, especially at British supermarkets such as Tesco and Sainsbury's. These include Shepherd Neame's malty Bishop's Finger (12.5%), John Smith's bitter (4.8% & 4%), Whitbread's creamy headed Boddington's bitter (3.8%), Tetley's creamy, nutty Yorkshire ale (3.6%) and Ireland's earthy, dry Guinness Draught (5%).

Whichever beer you choose your enjoyment will be heightened by the knowledge that it often costs only half of what you would have paid in the UK!

### Yes It's True -
### Beer from 12p per 25cl Bottle!
### Most outlets carry continental beers
### Here's a selection

| Beer | % Vol | Av. £ Price | Outlet |
|------|-------|-------------|--------|
| Munsterbrau | 4.7 | 12p | Auchan |
| Blondy | 5.0 | 13p | Pidou |
| Nordik Pils | 5.0 | 13p | Pidou |
| Blondebrau | 4.6 | 13p | Pidou |
| Seumeuse | 5.0 | 14p | Sainsbury's |
| St Omer 50cl cans per 25cl | 5.0 | 17p | Widely available |
| Sterling | 4.9 | 15 | Auchan |
| ESP | 5.2 | 17p | Eastenders |
| Kanterbrau | 4.7 | 18/19p | Widely available |
| Meteor Biere D'Alsace | 5.0 | 20p | Auchan |
| Kronenbourg | 4.7 | 21 p | Widely available |
| Stella Artois | 5.2 | 23p | Widely available |
| ESP | 9.2 | 24p | Eastenders |
| Amsterdam Mariner33cl | 5.0 | 26p | Widely available |
| 33 Export | 5.0 | 28p | Widely available |
| Grölsch | 5.0 | 29p | Widely available |
| 1664 | 6.3 | 30p | Widely available |

# Here For The Beer?

Incidentally...
An unlikely place for a
brewery is Cité Europe, the
huge shopping centre
situated in Coquelles,
Calais. Nevertheless this
shopping mall has its own
brew-pub. **Le Moulin à
Bière** is located on the
ground floor in the Cité
Gourmande area. The
brewing kettles are near the
bar behind which are the
fermentation tanks.  When
the beer is sufficiently
matured it is pumped directly
from the tanks to the bar
fountains for serving.

Incidentally...
The most popular selling
beer in Calais is St Omer
produced by the brewery
Brasserie de St. Omer.

Incidentally...
The beer most popularly
attributed with jump-starting
the revival of the French
brewing industry is Jenlain
Bière de Gard. It was first
brewed by Brasserie Duyck
in 1925 and by 1970 enjoyed
cult status with the student
population in Lille.

Incidentally...
In 1890 there were nearly
500 breweries in the Pas-de
Calais area. By 1985 just six
remained. Nowadays micro
brewing is back in fashion in
northern France. The
quaintest example of this is
the **Ferme-Brasserie Beck**
in the village of Bailleul. The
farm is owned and run by the
Beck family.

The Becks produce their own
dairy products and cereals
and raise horses and other
farm animals. The beer they
produce is called
**Hommelpap** (Flemish for
hops) and is a hefty 7% abv.
The farm is just half an
hour's drive from Calais and
a visit is recommended. You
can enjoy its delicious beer
with a simple dinner if you
visit on Saturday or Sunday
night between March and
September. There is also a
gîte in the grounds which
caters for large groups or a
party of friends who wish to
stay overnight.

**Brasserie Beck**
Eeckelstraete, 59270 Bailleu
Tel: 00 33 (0)3 28 49 0390.

# Here For The Beer?

Beer Labels: What do the terms on a beer label mean?

Abbey, Abbaye: This suggests a beer made by monks - not so, but the Trappist style has been used. Sometimes an abbey will have licensed it.

Ale: An English word meaning a brew made with a top-fermenting yeast - expect a certain fruitiness to its flavour

Bière de Gard: A French phrase for a top-fermented brew with an alcohol content between 4.4-7.5%.

Bitter: English word implying a depth of hop bitterness. The alcohol content is usually around 3.75-4%. If the word Best or Special is also present the alcohol content is slightly higher at 4-4.75%. The words Extra Special denote an alcohol content of 5.5%.

Export: In Germany this means a pale bottom-fermented beer with an alcohol content of 5.25-5.5%. Outside Germany this indicates a premium beer.

Ice Beer: The beer has been frozen at some stage.

Lager: Bottom-fermented beer.

Lambic: Wheat beer unique to Belgium. Alcohol content of 4.4%.

Pilsener/Pilsner/Pils: A term generally applied to golden coloured, dry, bottom-fermenting beer. A classic Pilsner is characterised by the hoppiness of its flowery aroma and dry finish. Its origins are in the Czech Republic from the town of Pilsen.

Stout: An extra-dark, top-fermenting brew made from roasted malts.

Trappist: An order of monks with five breweries in Belgium and one in the Netherlands. It is illegal to use this term for any other product. The beers are strong with an alcoholic content of 6-12%.

Tripel: Dutch word meaning the strongest beer of the house. Often pale in colour and top-fermented.

Weisse/Weissbier/Weizenbier: German for white beer.

# Eau, What A Choice!

**It's the best thirst quenching drink there is. It's not alcohol but it's a bargain !**

Mineral water (eau minérale) both still (plate) and sparkling (gazeuse) is exceptionally good value for money and substantially cheaper to buy in France. Why this is so is perplexing as unlike alcohol, there is no tax to blame.

There is often a vast selection of different brands at the hypermarkets. Some, such as Evian, Volvic and the comparatively expensive Perrier will be familiar, yet some of the lesser known brands are just as good. For example the sparkling River brand is just18p for 1.5 litres which we believe to be under half the price of the equivalent in the UK and Lucheux - which at 12.5p a 2-litre bottle must merit some space in your boot.

In our blind tasting, we sampled some mineral waters at fridge temperature. Here are a selection of commonly available waters:

**Badoit**: Slightly sparkling from the Loire.
Ave Price: 35p 1L Comment: Slightly salty
**Contrexéville**: From Vosges. Reputedly good for the kidneys. Has a slightly diuretic effect.
Ave Price: 3p) 1.5L Comment: Slightly salty.
**Evian**: From the town of Evian on Lake Geneva.It has a slightly diuretic effect.
Ave Price: 42p 2L Comment: Tasteless but thirst quenching.
**Perrier**: A well marketed mineral water from Nîmes. Full of sparkle and is generally used as soda water in France.
Ave Price: 45p 1L Comment: Most refreshing with almost no flavour.
**River**: Sparkling water
Ave Price:18p 1.5L Comment: Slightly chalky on the palate.
**Vichy**: A sparkler from Vichy.
Ave Price: 30p 1.5L Comment: Like bicarbonate of soda.
**Vittel**: A still yet rugged mineral water from Nancy.
Ave Price: 28p 1.5L Comment: Refreshing and slightly sweet.
**Volvic**: A still water from the Auvergne filtered through volcanic rock.
Ave Price: 30p 1.5L Comment: Smooth silky taste.

# The Epicurean's Tour of The Shops

When shopping in any French town what stands out is the variety of traditional gastronomic shops, some of which have no comparable counterpart in the UK. It must be a cultural thing but, very simply, the French like to specialise.

Take the Boucherie for example - the butcher. The Boucherie sells all types of meat and poultry - except pork. To buy pork you need to visit the Charcuterie - which means cooked meat.

The Charcuterie, originally a pork butcher, has evolved into a pork-based delicatessen. Visiting a Charcuterie for the first time will shift your perception of the humble pig "le cochon' in gastro-nomic terms for ever! Now you will see it as pâté, terrien, rillettes, illons, hams, dried sausages, fresh sausages, ieds de porc, ndouillettes, boudins noirs t blancs. This pork lover's haven also offers ready made pork meals with a selection of plats du jour

that just need heating up when you get home.

Horse meat is also popular in France and this is sold in outlets known as Boucherie Chevaline - horse meat butcher, generally identifiable by a horse's head sign.

Cheese, a much revered commodity in France, is produced with exacting procedures by the highly skilled maître fromager (master cheese specialist). The shop to visit to get the feel of the cheese culture at its best is the Fromagerie - a specialist cheese shop which will probably have around 300 varieties on sale.

A cross between a grocery store and a delicatessen is the Epicerie. The store sells cheese and fresh meat among other food products. These days the Epricerie is based a little on the Supermarché and an Alimentation Général - a general store - and has lost some of its authenticity.

# The Epicurean's Tour of The Shops

Calais and Boulogne both being fishing towns are awash with fresh seafood. You can buy the catch of the day from the Poissonerie. This could be a fishmonger or just a stall.

Another example of specialisation in action is the Boulangerie - the bakery. The shelves are stacked with all types of unusual bread and buns and occasionally cakes and quiches too.

But for a fiendishly good selection of cakes and biscuits, it is over to the Pâtisserie for specialist cake, flans and tarts. The Pâtisserie sometimes sells ice cream too.

Sweets, not the commercial pre-wrapped type, but handmade sweets such as bon-bons, nougat and crystallised fruit, have their own home in a Confiserie or Chocolaterie - a high class sweet or chocolate shop. The products are a little pricey but good quality, delicious and beautifully packaged.

For fresh fruit, flowers and vegetables and fresh French delights the best place is the Marché - outdoor market. These are generally open on a Saturday or Wednesday.

You could of course by-pass the specialist shops which offer pleasant insightful echoes of French daily life and culture - a shopping experience unlike any you can have in the UK. You could, instead shop in one of the immense Hypermarché - hypermarkets. The total anonymity that comes with being one of hundreds of trolley pushers walking around thousands of kilometres of floor space in a state of suspended reality is an experience all of its own!

# Say Cheese

**Take a glass of your favourite wine, break off a piece of baguette, fill it with your favourite cheese - voila! a slice of French culture.**

The inherent passion for wine within the French culture is closely followed by love for cheese, so much so that France has become renowned for its remarkably large choice of cheeses. Incredibly, the number of different varieties is believed to be in excess of 700. Not only do supermarkets dedicate large areas of floor space to their cheese counters, but the French also have specialist cheese shops.

These quaint shops are called Fromageries offering cheese in all its colours and consistencies.

Though nasal passages have to grapple with the pungent aroma that hangs heavily in the air, the palate can look forward to a delightful epicurean experience. It is at the fromagerie that the finest cheeses can be found, thanks to the resident maître fromager. His highly skilled job combines the complexities of cheese selection, storage and the delicate process of "affinage'. This is the art of ageing a young cheese to maturity so that it is offered in its prime.

To the uninitiated though, the cheese counter must look like a daunting display of yellow and white hues with the odd shout of blue. No matter how tempting these colours look, one wonders about the taste. Fortunately, it is customary for supermarkets and fromageries to offer dégustation (sampling) upon request.

Fromageries to try are:

**La Maison du Fromage,** 1 rue Andre-Gerschel, Calais: **show your guide and for every £10 you spend get 5% off**.
In Boulogne you can try **La Cave du Fromager**, 23 rue de Lille.

In Dunkerque try **Cremerie La Ferme** at 22 rue Poincaré.

Boulogne is especially favoured with **Phillippe Oliver's** cheese shop at 43 rue Thiers, reputedly the most famous cheese vendor in the world. Philippe Olivier has created a heavenly cave of cheese and a visit here is a must for any cheese lover.

Although it is not possible to list all available cheeses, some will already be familiar to you, such as Normandy's camembert and brie from Ile de France (especially the President label) are widely found and at a third less than UK prices. Fromages fermiers (farmhouse cheese) are considered to be the finest of all. These are made by small producers using milk from their own farm animals. When unpasteurised milk is used this is denoted with the words "lait cru'. Other varieties to try are:

Le Brin. A small hexagon shaped cheese. Made from cow's milk, it is mild and creamy. The edible rind has a delicate, pleasant aroma. The special method of production leaves the cheese high in calcium and phosphorus.

Cantorel Roquefort. A speciality of southwest France, this blue cheese is ripened in the caves of Cambalou for at least 90 days in accordance with its Appellation d'Origine Contrôlée. Made entirely from sheep's milk, its distinctive taste is best enjoyed with Barsac or Sauternes wines.

Chimay. You may already be familiar with the Belgian Trappist beer of this name Chimay is also a range of six Belgian Trappist cheeses. Chimay Bière is flavoured with the beer and is a treat for the palate.

Rambol. Decorated with walnuts it looks like a small gâteau and is smooth with a mellow flavour.

Société Roquefort. Creamy in texture and distinguished by its marbled green and ivory colouring.

# Say Cheese

St Agur. A creamy blue veined cheese from the Auvergne. It has a mild flavour and sits well on a cheese board.

Tartare. A cream cheese spread from Périgord made with garlic and herbs. It comes as a full fat cheese and for slimmers there's Tartare Light with just a third of the calorie content.

Trappe de Belval. Made by nuns at the abbey of Belval located near Hesdin. It has a rather hard exterior concealing a creamy and mild interior.

## Serving suggestions:

- Cheese is at its best served at room temperature. Remove from the fridge at least one hour before required.
- Allow 2oz per person for a cheese board and 4oz per person for a cheese and wine evening.
- Select 3-4 different types of cheese for an attractive display, especially on a cheese board.

## Storage Tips:

Fortunately, most hard cheeses can be frozen as long as they are not overmature. This is not recommended for soft cheeses.

Generally, the following guidelines for fridge storage apply:

- Fresh Cheese (soft cheese): Eat within a few days.
- Blue Cheese Can be kept up to three weeks.
- Goat's Ewe's Milk Cheese: Will keep for up to two weeks.
- Always store cheese in the lowest part of the fridge wrapped in foil or in an air proof container to prevent drying out.

Fromagerie

# French Bread

*It's the law! Every French village must have its own boulangerie (bakery) supplying the villagers with freshly baked bread every day of the week.*

Governed by French law, the boulangerie emerges as the single most important shop in any village, faithfully providing the residents with an essential part of their staple diet - bread.

As with all things French an etiquette has evolved around bread. It is generally considered unacceptable to serve in the evening bread purchased in the morning. No self-respecting Frenchman would dare to insult his guests in this way!

*Boulangerie at Carrefour*

However, left-over bread may be used perhaps for dunking in hot chocolate - in specially formulated wide cups - or alternatively can be cooked in soup.

The most famous and popular French bread (both within and outside France) is the long, thin baguette or French stick. It is uniform in length and its weight - governed by French law - must be 250 grams!

Although the baguette is made simply from soft flour, yeast, water and a pinch or two of salt, it has an appealing fluffy texture and can be enjoyed just as well on its own as it can with food. However, its short life span means that it must be consumed soon after it has been baked. Bakeries routinely bake bread twice a day to ensure fresh loaves for a very discriminating public.

Other extreme variations on the baguette are the ficelle

(which means string). It is the thinnest loaf available. In contrast un pain or Pariesen is double the size of a baguette. A compromise is reached with petit pains and the bâtons which are much shorter than the baguette and similar to large rolls. For breakfast (le petit dèjeuner) the French will also enjoy a continental breakfast (better known in France as viennoiserie). This includes such delicious treats as the famous pastry-style croissant. This familiar crescent-shaped roll was Marie Antoinett's inadvertent contribution to western breakfast culture. She introduced them to Parisian royals in the late 18th century where they proved to be an epicurean hit.

In Marie Antoinette's home country of Vienna, however, the croissant had been making a regular appearance at the breakfast table as early as 1683. It was in this year that the Polish army saved the city from Turkish hands and in celebration the Viennese baked a crescent-shaped creation based on the Ottoman flag - voila, the croissant was born!

The croissant is similar to puff pastry - made with yeast dough and butter and is usually accompanied by confit (crystallised fruit) or confiture (various flavours of jam). Sometimes it is served with jam, cheese or chocolate and can be savoured hot or cold.

Traditionally, the croissant is dunked by the French into their coffee in  wide cups designed for this purpose. This French idiosyncrasy can also be traced back to the late 17th century. The defeated Turks had left some sacks of coffee beans before they left Vienna. These were discovered by a group of Armenian Jews who started the croissant dunking tradition.

There are also many other tempting and unusual styles of bread available at the specialist boulangerie (bakery) or the boulangerie counter of the hypermarket.

Here are some suggestions you may like to try:

**Pain au chocolat** a croissant style bun imbued with chocolate (delicious when warm).

**Brioche** a breakfast bun made from yeast, dough, eggs and butter, giving it a wonderful sweet, buttery aroma and taste.

**Couronnes**. a baguette style bread in the shape of a ring.

**Pain aux noix** an outstanding bread baked with walnuts on the inside and on the crust.

**Pain aux olives** a delicious bread with olives and olive oil.

**Pain de sègle** made with rye and wheat.

**Pain noir** wholemeal bread.

**Pain de son** wholemeal bread fortified with bran.

**Pain de mie** sliced bread with a soft crust. Used for sandwiches.

**Pain biologique** this bread is baked with organic wholemeal flour.

**Pain campagne** flatter than a baguette but also heavier. It has the advantage of staying fresh for longer.

**Pain au Levain/Pain à l'ancienne** both these names refer to French bread made from sour dough. This is probably one of the oldest styles of French bread.

# Specialities at the Pâtisserie

**_If, like the French, you have a sweet tooth
then a visit to a pâtisserie gives a
whole new meaning to the phrase
"Let Them Eat Cake"_**

In true French style, even the last course of a meal is not the least. Dinner in any French home will always conclude with a sweet, which if not home made will be bought from the pâtisserie - a specialist cake shop. The pâtisserie may also have a selection of handmade confectionary.

Like French wines and cheese, different areas of France have their own regional indulgences on offer. For instance, from Provence come Marrons Glacés and Fruits Glacés: the former is an autumnal treat of chestnuts in vanilla-flavoured syrup; the latter is fresh fruit in sugar syrup.

Normandy, famous for its apple orchards, offers Tarte Normande. A variation is Gratin de Pommes Vallée D'Auge - it is no ordinary apple crumble; it is soaked in calvados (an apple brandy produced in Normandy) and then baked in crème fraîche. The Pas de Calais also has an indigenous tart whose thick pastry has led to the name Tarte au Gros Bord. It is adorned simply with custard and sugar.

Other offerings include:

**Anglois**
A simple plum tart.

**Biscuit de Reims**
A small oblong shaped macaroon from Reims.

**Galopin**
A thick pancake sprinkled with sugar.

**Gaufres à la Flamande -**
Waffles powdered with sugar and sometimes served with whipped cream.

**Pain d'épices**
A spicey honey cake.

# Specialities at the Pâtisserie

**Rabote**
A whole apple cooked in pastry.

**Tarte au Fromage**
Cheese cake made from eggs and cottage cheese.

**Nougat Glacé**
From Provence a frozen honey and almond desert.

**Pastis Gascon**
Thin pastry, layered between the folds with vanilla sugar and butter, adorned with apple and marinated in armagnac.

**Baba au Rhum** - A yeast product soaked in rum flavoured syrup. Best eaten with a spoon.

**Where to shop for your bread and cakes:**

Joly Desenclos
46 rue de Lille
6220 Boulogne sur Mer
Tel: 00 33 (0)3 21 80 50 52

Fred
Boulevard Jacquard
Calais
Situated near the Town Hall with a tea room.

Pâtisserie Boutteau
19 place Jean-Bart
Dunkerque
Tel: 00 33 (0)3 28 66 77 81
A family run business established in 1892 with a tea room,

La Croissantine
84 bis, rue St Jean
Le Touquet
Tel: 00 33 (0)3 21 06 30 50

# Foie Gras

**The Egyptians enjoyed it more than 2000 years ago. So did the ancient Greeks and Roman emperors. The French perfected it into an art form during the last 200 years and now you can enjoy it too.**

Foie gras, pronounced *fwah gra*, is a much revered goose liver pâté. It means *fat liver*. In winter, the geese are force-fed with corn and grain so that their livers become supple and enlarged to produce large quantities of *foie* - liver.

Foie gras is sometimes augmented with truffles but either way it is available cooked or semi-cooked in tins or jars. The latter condition gives it a longer shelf life in the refrigerator.

Serve it thoroughly chilled but slice it with a warmed knife. Accompany it with toast or baguette and enjoy a truly gastronomic taste of France.

**Where to buy foie gras**

**L'Epicerie Des Dunes**
corner of Faidherbe and Geeraert
Dunkerque Malo
Tel: 00 33 (0)3 28 63 22 09

**Comtesse du Barry**
59 Boulevard Jacquard
Calais
Tel: 00 33 (0)3 21 85 14 13

**Comtesse du Barry**
35 Grande Rue
Boulogne
Tel: 00 33 (0)3 21 87 19 20

**Marché Plus**
70 rue de Metz
Le Touquet
Tel: 00 33 (0)3 21 05 03 89

**Sauternes wine is a divine accompaniment to Foie Gras**

# Calais Lace

***Everyone knows about Calais lace. But did you know it was started by English smugglers?***

According to French chronicles, the first Englishman to smuggle a lace machine into Calais was Robert Webster in 1816. Though the reliability of this reporting cannot be verified, it is a fact that illegal smuggling of lace machines by Englishmen into Calais did take place. In Blighty, Nottingham lace makers were plying their trade by hand. To them, modern technology meant unemployment. Opposition was so bitter that the machines were smuggled to Calais where conditions were more welcoming. The English set up home in terraced houses-cum-workshops in the Calais district of St Pierre. Unemployment in the area was high so finding workers was easy. Import taxes were also high so they had little competition from their counterparts in England. Most importantly, the French aristocracy had returned to Calais and loved the luxurious lace.

In fact, the entire industry developed so well in the hands of expatriate Englishmen that Calais become internationally reknowned for its fashionable, quality lace. Even today, a hefty 78% of the lace production in Calais is exported to 140 countries around the world (and 80% of that is made into lingerie!).

The lace industry in Calais is still run by families, many of whom are of English descent. Though they are inherently French, they still eat Christmas pudding and welsh-rarebit

---

**Where to buy lace in Calais**

**Royal-Dentelle:
62 rue Royale
00 33 (0)3 21 97 57 64**

# Tobacco Prices Up In Smoke!

**With savings of £2.00 or more on a packet of cigarettes, topping up in France makes sense.**

| Product | France | U.K. |
|---|---|---|
| | Av. £ | Av. £ |
| **Cigarettes** | Av. £ | Av. £ |
| Benson & Hedges | £2.06 | £4.20 |
| Camel | £2.29 | £4.20 |
| Dunhill | £2.72 | £4.20 |
| Gauloises | £2.46 | £3.90 |
| Gitanes | £1.74 | £4.20 |
| John Player Special | £1.80 | £3.70 |
| Lambert & Butler | £2.23 | £4.00 |
| Marlboro | £2.34 | £4.20 |
| Rothmans | £2.15 | £4.20 |
| Silk Cut | £2.34 | £4.20 |
| Superkings | £2.23 | £3.60 |
| | | |
| **Tobacco** | | |
| Drum 50g | £2.66 | £7.00 |
| Golden Virginia 40g | £2.08 | £7.47 |
| Old Holborn 40g | £2.34 | £7.47 |
| Samson 50g | £2.30 | £7.37 |
| | | |
| **Cigars x 5** | | |
| King Edward Imperial | £4.00 | £8.90 |
| Villager Export | £3.75 | £4.60 |

You can in theory buy unlimited amounts of tobacco for personal use both on board the ferries or in France but the "advisory guideline" is 800 cigarettes. In France, tobacco can be purchased from Tabacs where prices are state regulated. Not so in petrol stations where prices are higher. Unlike the UK, French supermarkets do not sell tobacco at all.Most tabacs are closed on Sundays and bank holidays but most accept credit cards. In general you can expect savings of around 50% when you buy cigarettes on board the ferries. You can expect to save a further 5% when you buy them in Tabacs

# Other Shopping Ideas

**With the pound so strong, shopping in France is altogether cheaper these days.**
**Here are some shopping comparisons**

## Le Shopping Basket

| Product | Av. France £ | Av. UK £ |
|---|---|---|
| Butter (cheapest brand) | £0.26 | £0.72 |
| Brie (1 kilo) | £2.81 | £3.12 |
| Petit Filou Fromage Frais x 18pots | £1.50 | £2.55 |
| Nutella Chocolate spread 400g | £1.09 | £1.66 |
| Long Grain Rice 1kg | £0.54 | £1.00 |
| Cous Cous kg | £0.65 | £1.20 |
| Pasta 1kg | £0.52 | £0.96 |
| Kellogs Cornflakes 375g | £1.00 | £1.39 |
| Pork per 1.5kg | £3.74 | £5.08 |
| Stewing steak 1kg | £5.50 | £6.06 |
| Evian Still water1.5L | £0.47 | £0.67 |
| Nesquick 430ml | £1.10 | £2.49 |
| 1 bottle of white wine | £2.00 | £4.00 |
| 1 x 2L Coca-Cola | £0.85 | £1.17 |
| Carte Noir Arabica Coffee 250g | £6.19 | £7.89 |
| Lavazza Espresso 250g | £1.65 | £1.99 |
| Fruit Juice 1L carton | £0.43 | £0.85 |
| Aluminium Foil 20mx290m | £1.34 | £2.09 |
| Kitchen roll (pack of 2 own brand) | £0.70 | £1.39 |
| Persil Washing Biological Powder 7.2kg | £8.42 | £11.30 |
| Domestos Bleach 75cl | £2.27 | £2.69 |
| Cif/Jif Bathroom Cleaning Cream per L | £1.62 | £2.50 |
| Ajax Spray bathroom spray 500ml | £1.20 | £1.60 |
| Own label dishwasher tablets | £3.04 | £4.97 |
| Toilet rolls (pack of 6 own brand) | £1.00 | £1.90 |
| Gillette Sensor Razor blades 5pk | £0.32 | £0.89 |
| Gillette Sensor Excel Shaving Razor | £2.33 | £3.89 |
| Sensodyne toothpaste 75ml | £1.90 | £2.50 |
| Two torch batteries | £2.80 | £3.49 |
| **Totals** | **£57.24** | **£82.01** |

Save across the ocean at **Auchan**

FOOD • CLOTHING • ELECTRICAL GOODS

# Save up to
# 30%
## on UK high street prices

**Auchan Hypermarket in Calais
is the only place to shop.
Everything's under one roof.**

**Fill up your car with unleaded petrol at
Auchan Calais. You can save about
£10 compared to an average UK tank price**

GARDENING • KITCHENWARE • LUGGAGE • TOYS

g Times:
y to Saturday 08.30-22.00
y 25 November
2, 9, 16 & 23 December 08.30-20.00

**From the tunnel:**
Straight on to A16 direction Calais
Centre. Exit Junction 12. Follow
signs for Auchan and Sainsbury's.

**From the ferry/hoverport:**
Join A16 and follow signs for
Boulogne. Exit Junction 12. Follow
signs for Auchan and Sainsbury's.

# Other Shopping Ideas

## Fish (Poisson)
If you have enjoyed a fish or seafood meal, you may be inclined to buy your own to take home. Hypermarkets have a comprehensive fish and seafood section or better still, visit a fish monger (poissonnerie).

## Peanuts (Cacahuètes)
30% cheaper than the UK.

## Mustard (Moutard)
Dijon mustard prices start at 22p for 370g jar of Dijon mustard compared to a typical UK price of 59p for 250g. English mustard is slightly hotter. Try seeded Dijon mustard; it has a particularly delicate flavour.

## Anchovies
You get a wider selection of anchovies, and at half price in France.

## Olives
In general olives (both black and green) are about 30% cheaper in France.

## Olive Oil (Huile d'olives)
The finest French olive oils - like French wines - come from named origins and *Appellations Contrôlées*.

They have a gentle flavour tempered with slight sweetness and are great as condiments, but not suitable for cooking.

These olive oils have low acidity (sometimes as little as 0.2%) which is significant because acidity affects the rate at which the oil deteriorates. Labels of assured finest quality to look out for are Huile de Provence and Huile d'Olives Nyons (the latter is subject to quality control with its own Appellation d'Origine. This sort of quality is expensive and could be up to £30.00 in the UK (less in France). Generally, you are likely to buy commercially blended brands.

Look for either Extra Virgin (Vierge) or First Cold Pressing (Premier Presson Froid) whose acidity is never more than 1%, but is better still at 0.5%, Fine Virgin olive oil at 1.5% or less, and Ordinary Virgin olive oil whose acidity level is 3%. This sort of quality olive oil in the UK is rarely below £6.00 per litre, yet in France the price is around £3.50.

# Other Shopping Ideas

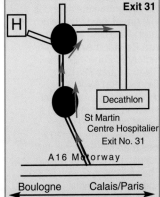

# Other Shopping Ideas

## Cider (Cidre)

French supermarkets and some cash & carries, sell both French and UK ciders. There are differences, notably that French cider tends to contain less alcohol, around 2.4% as opposed to 5%+ for the British ciders. British ciders such as Strongbow and Bulmers are generally available in France at about half the UK price.

## Glassware

Duralex, Luminarc and Cristal D'Arques are names you may already be familiar with. They are available in the hypermarkets at prices that are at least 20% less than in the UK. You can visit **Cristal d'Arques'** factory at Zone Industrielle, RN43 Arques 62510, Tel: 00 33 321 93 46 96 (A26 motorway, Arques exit). There is a museum and a visitor centre and shop. Prices are generally 20% less than the French retail outlets, but call in advance. The visit costs around £3.00 and includes a gift.

## Light Bulbs

Not a huge saving to be made, but 15% is enough to bring a little light.

## Tissues

Both boxed and handbag size are at least 25% cheaper across the board.

## Batteries

Around 20% cheaper in the hypermarkets.

## Tiles

Tiles are generally 25%-35% cheaper in France. For a really good range, you could try Hurtrel. It stocks ceramic, kitchen, bathroom and exterior and interior floor tiles. Hurtrel are offering another

### 15% off prices exclusively for Channel Hoppers.

So if you are in the market, this is the place to visit. Be prepared though - you will need a van.

WE HAVE BEEN SERVING OUR
BRITISH CUSTOMERS FOR 30 YEARS

12 specialised stores
1 shopping mall
4 restaurants
A 24-hour petrol station
with a camper service station

**A16**

Direction Boulogne

Exit 31

**31**

direction
St. Omer

**Auchan**
Côte d'Opale

TEL : 00 33 3 21 10 11 12 - FAX : 00 33 3 21 10 11 26

## Mountain Bikes (VTT)

Although we are unable to give a true comparison on mountain bikes, we can say that the hypermarkets do have good value ones. Adult mountain bikes start at under £100 and children's mountain bikes can be found for around £40. It is difficult to find these prices in UK.

## Garden Furniture (Jardinage)

Garden furniture is often half the UK price of the equivalent and tempting to buy - but you will need a lot of space in your car! At Leroy Merlin (next to Auchan), Continent, Carrefour and Auchan there is a good selection of both plastic and pine table and chair sets. Plastic chairs start from £2.50 and plastic tables 85cm in diameter from as little as £14.90. A pine table and chair set can be found for only £75.00.

Garden parasols are also around £10.00 cheaper in France.

## Pots and Pans

You may already be familiar with the names Le Creuset and Tefal. These two popular quality brands of pots and pans are both manufactured in France. You can purchase these in the hypermarkets and supermarkets for as little as half the UK price. For example, the Le Creuset 20cm saucepan is typically sold in the UK for around £33.00 yet it is available at French hypermarkets at around £15.50.

## Baby's Furniture

Furniture for babies is considerably less in france:

| | |
|---|---|
| Prams - | 25% less |
| High chairs - | 25% less |
| Bouncy chairs - | 35% less |
| Travel cots - | 50% less |
| Car seats - | 55% less |

---

**Do you know something we don't?**
Tell us about it and you could get a free copy the The Channel Hopper's Guide

---

# Other Shopping Ideas

TIP:
Serious bargain hunters should time their trip with the French sales. These happen twice a year - in January and in August and generally last between one to two months. You can pick up some fantastic bargains!

TIP:
In August Calais becomes a huge outdoor flea market known as the Braderie.

TIP:
Take a cooler bag with you just in case you want to buy fresh products such as cheese or fish to maintain freshness and avoid any pungent smells on the journey home.

Tip:
Shops close at lunch time.

Tip:
Cat food, baked beans, tomato ketchup, sliced bread, margarine, tuna, frozen pizza, air freshener, nappies and most branded soap are actually more expensive in France!

**Othcr Types of Shops on the High Street.**

Alimentation Général:
General store

Pharmacie:
Chemist that sells primarily medicines

Droguerie:
Related to the hardware store, selling primarily toiletries

Nettoyage à sec:
Dry cleaners

Carrelages
Sells tiles

Tabac:
Tobacconist, the only shop that sells cigarettes and tobacco. Also sells stamps

Maison de la Presse
Sells magazines and newspapers

Librarie:
Book shop

Quincaillerie:
Hardware store

# Eating Out

*Everything stops for lunch in France. Take time out to enjoy a pastime the French take very seriously - eating!*

You know lunchtime has arrived in France when you see the sign 'fermé' (closed) on shop doors. As the shops and factories close, the restaurants open for business offering a choice of cuisine and ambience.

French culinary diversity is very much inspired by the country's variety of landscape and locally farmed produce. Generally three distinct styles of cuisine are evident:

Haute Cuisine
The hallmarks of Haute Cuisine are its rich food and elaborate presentation. This style can be tracked back to Louis XIV's 12-hour feasts in the Palace of Versailles.

Cuisine Bourgeoise
This style is related to Haute Cuisine. Less elaborate perhaps and best described as high quality home cooking.

Nouvelle Cuisine
This trendy cooking style originated in the 1970s. The dishes are generally less rich, fresh ingredients are used and vegetables are al dente - almost raw - to optimise their natural flavours and aromas.

Choosing a restaurant is easy as they generally display their menus outside. Steer clear of empty restaurants - in our experience, they generally deserve to be so! If you have booked a table be sure to be on time, as it is unlikely to be saved for more than ten minutes, especially on Sundays when everyone ikes to eat out en famille.

Most restaurants cater for tourists by offering a menu touristique usually written in English or with an English translation alongside the regional dishes. This is often good

# Eating Out

value for money and comprises such dishes as steak and French fries.

One item that will be missing from any French menu is the traditional two-slices-of-bread British sandwich. You may find it referred to on the menu at cafés or brasseries, but it will never be served in sliced bread. The most popular sandwich is the croque monsieur which is basically ham and cheese in a ficelle (a slimmer version of a baguette). The feminine version of this is croque madame which comes with a fried egg too.

Alternatively, you could choose the Prix Fixe menu, a set price menu which may include the plat du jour (dish of the day) or spécialité de la maison (house special). These are a better choice for those wishing to try a local dish, usually seafood or frogs' legs, cuisses de grenouilles. Indulge in the à la carte menu or the menu gastronomique for finer quality food.

Not all prices will be highlighted on the menu. The letters SG may sit alongside some dishes and stand for selon grosseur (according to weight). This applies to dishes that, for practical purposes, are sold by weight, such as lobster or fish. In this instance it is advisable to find out the price before you order.

If the words service compris (service included) or service et taxes compris (service and taxes included) are on the menu, that means the prices include a service charge. However, odd coins are usually left for the waiter. Otherwise, a 10% tip is customary.

Meals are never rushed in restaurants even if you only want a snack and a drink at one of the cafés. You can while away the time at your leisure but if you are eating to a deadline, pay for your meal when it arrives, as catching the waiter's eye later may prove a challenge.

### *Make no mistake...*
### *a steak is rare*
### *whichever way you ask for it!*

Like most nations, France is peopled with carnivores. There is nothing unusual in that. However, it helps to know that when it comes to steak, the meat is invariably served rare.

The concept of medium or well done is not one easily understood by the typical French chef; he is more comfortable preparing the steak in differing degrees of rare. The reason for this is found in the national belief that the meat is more tender, tastes better and better for the health if served rare.

If ordering steak in a restaurant, you will generally be asked if you like your steak **saignant** or **à point**. If neither appeal, you will have to be assertive and asked for it to be **bien, bien cuit** and hope for a medium done steak.

**Steak terms:**

**Bleue**
The meat has been cooked for barely two minutes and the meat has vaguely changed colour.

**Saignant**
The meat has been cooked for for two or more minutes but the meat is still 'bleeding' red juices.

**A Point**
Considered medium done in France, but in truth the meat is rare.

**Bien Cuit**
This means well done France, but in truth the steak is rare verging on medium.

**Steak Tartare**
Raw minced beef thoroughly mixed together with a raw egg yolk.

# Eating Out

Tip: Go for French food while in France. This not only adds to the French experience, but also makes good economic sense; traditional British food and drink such as tea, Scotch whisky and gin or a plate of bacon and eggs are expensive. So check out the menu or tarif des consommations (if in a café or bar) for something that tickles your palate and accompany it with wine (vin ordinaire) or draught beer (pression).

French spirits and soft drinks are generally an inexpensive relative to their British counterparts on the menu.

Tip: To get the attention of the waiter lift your index finger and call Monsieur - not garçon. A waitress should be addressed as Madame or Mademoiselle.

Tip: Do not ask for a doggy bag. This concept simply does not exist in France.

Tip: When ordering coffee, be specific and say exactly what you would like. Unlike British restaurants, just ordering a coffee will not do because the French have a different idea of how it should be served. They will serve coffee strong and black, espresso style as standard. The exception to this is during the breakfast meal when coffee is served in large wide-mouthed coffee cups - specially designed for dunking - and milk is a standard accompaniment.

Coffee Styles

Un café, s'il vous plaît
You will receive an espresso coffee, strong and black in a small espresso cup

Un café au lait s'il vous plaît
You will receive an espresso coffee with milk on the side.

Une crème s'il vous plaît
You will receive a small white coffee

Une crème grande s'il vous plaît
You will receive a white coffee served in a normal size cup.

# Eating Out

## Terms on a French Menu

| Le Viandes | Meat | Les Poissons | Fish |
|---|---|---|---|
| L'Agneau | Lamb | Anchois | Anchovy |
| Assiette | Plate of | Anguille | Eel |
| Anglaise | cold meats | Araignée | Spider Crab |
| Bifteck | Steak | L'Assiette | Smoked Fish |
| Bifteck Haché | Hamburger | Nordique | Platter |
| Boeuf | Beef | Bar et Loup de | |
| Carré d'Agneau | Rib of Lamb | Mer | Sea-wolf |
| Chevreuil | Venison | Barbe | Brill |
| Côtes | Lamb | Bigorneau | Winkle |
| d'Agneau | Chops | Cabillaud | Fresh Cod |
| Côte de Boeuf | Side of Beef | Carrelet et Plie | Plaice |
| Côte de Porc | Pork Chop | Colin | Hake |
| Côte de Veau | Veal | Coquilles St- | |
| Contrefilet | Sirloin | Jacques | Scallops |
| Entrecôte | Steak | Crabes | Crabs |
| Faux Filet | Sirloin Steak | Crevette Grise | Shrimp |
| Filet de Boeuf | Fillet of Beef | Crustacés | Shellfish |
| Foie | Liver | Dorade | Sea Bream |
| Foie de Veau | Calves' Liver | Ecrevisses | Crayfish |
| Gigot d'Agneau | Leg of Lamb | Escargots | Snails |
| Jambon | Ham | Etrille | Swimming Cra |
| Langue | Tongue | Fruit de Mer | Seafood |
| Langue de Boeuf | Ox Tongue | Gamba | Large Prawn |
| Lapin | Rabbit | Harengs | Herring |
| Lard Fumé | Smoked Bacon | Homard | Lobster |
| Lièvre | Hare | Limande | Lemon Sole |
| Porc | Pork | Langouste | Spiny Lobster |
| Rognons | Kidneys | Langoustines | Norway Lobste |
| Saucisse | Sausage | Huître | Oyster |
| Tête de Veau | Calves' Head | Lieu | Coal Fish |

# Eating Out

| Les Poissons | Fish contd. |
|---|---|
| Limande | Lemon Sole |
| Maquereau | Mackerel |
| Merlan | Whiting |
| Morue | Cod |
| Moules | Mussels |
| Péntoncle | Small Scallop |
| Praire | Clam |
| Raie | Skate |
| Rouget | Red Mullet |
| Salad Océan | Ocean Salad |
| Sardines | Sardines |
| Saumon | Salmon |
| Sole | Sole |
| Thon | Tuna |
| Truite (de Mer) | Trout (Sea) |
| Truite arc en ciel | Rainbow Trout |
| Turbot | Turbot |

| Volaille | Poultry |
|---|---|
| Caneton/Canard | Duck |
| Caille | Quail |
| Dindon | Turkey |
| Oie | Goose |
| Faisan | Pheasant |
| Foie Gras | Duck Liver pâté |
| Foie Volaille | Chicken Liver |
| Lotte | Monkfish |
| Magret Canard | Duck Fillet |
| Perdreau | Partridge |
| Pigeon | Pigeon |
| Poulet | Chicken |

| | |
|---|---|
| Poularde | Boiled Chicken |
| Poussin | Spring Chicken |
| Ris de Veau | Veal sweetbread |

| Sauce | Sauce |
|---|---|
| Béarnaise | Sauce made from egg yolks, shallots, wine and tarragon |
| Béchamel | White sauce with herbs |
| Beurre Blanc | Loire sauce with butter, wine and shallots |
| Beurre Noir | Blackened butter |
| Meunière | Butter and lemon sauce |

## How do you like your eggs?

| Oeufs | Eggs |
|---|---|
| - Coque | - Boiled |
| - Brouillés | - Scrambled |
| - Pochés | - Poached |
| Oeufs sur le plat | Fried eggs |

### A-Z of Miscellaneous French Menu Terms

| French | English | French | English |
|---|---|---|---|
| Abricots | Apricots | Cresson | Cress |
| Amandes | Almonds | Croustade | Tartlets |
| Ananas | Pineapple | Cuit au Four | Baked |
| Araignée | Spider-crab | Endives | Chicory |
| Artichaut | Artichoke | Epinards | Spinach |
| Asperge | Asparagus | Estragon | Tarragon |
| Aubergines | Aubergines | Farine | Flour |
| Avocat | Avocado | Fenouil | Fennel |
| Bécasse | Woodcock | Fèves | Beans |
| Betteraves | Beetroot | Figues | Figs |
| Beurre | Butter | Flageolets | Kidney Beans |
| Braisé | Braised | Fraises | Strawberry |
| Brochette | Skewer | Framboises | Raspberries |
| Brouillade | Stew with oil | Fromage Blanc | Cream Cheese |
| Caille | Quail | Fromage Chèvre | Goats' Cheese |
| Carottes | Carrots | Fromages | Cheeses |
| Céleri | Celery | Fumé | Smoked |
| Cerises | Cherries | Gratinée | Grill browned |
| Champignons | Mushrooms | Grenouilles | Frogs |
| Châtaignes | Chestnuts | Grillé | Grilled |
| Chicorée | Chicory | Groseilles | Currants |
| Choux Bruxelle | Brussel Sprout | Harricots Verts | French Beans |
| Chou Rouge | Red Cabbage | Laitue | Lettuce |
| Chou vert | Kale | Mais | Sweet Corn |
| Choux Fleurs | Cauliflowers | Mandarines | Mandarines |
| Citron | Lemon | Marron | Chestnut |
| Concombre | Cucumber | Melon | Melon |
| Consommé | Clear soup | Navets | Turnips |
| Courgettes | Courgette | Noisettes | Hazelnuts |
| Crème Glacée | Ice cream | Noix | Walnuts |
| Crêpes | Pancakes | | |

| | |
|---|---|
| Oie | Goose |
| Oignons | Onions |
| Oseille | Sorrel |
| Oursins | Sea Hedgehog |
| Pastèque | Water Melon |
| Pêches | Peaches |
| Petits Pois | Green Peas |
| Pintade | Guinea-fowl |
| Pissenlits | Dandelions |
| Poire | Pear |
| Poivre | Pepper |
| Poireaux | Leeks |
| Poivrons rouges | Red Pepper |
| Poivrons Verts | Green Pepper |
| Pomme de Terre | Potato |
| Pomme | Apple |
| Potage | Soup |
| Prunes | Prunes |
| Radis | Radishes |
| Railfort | Horse Radish |
| Raisins | Grapes |
| Reine-Claude | Greengages |
| Riz | Rice |
| Rôti | Roasted |
| Sel | Salt |
| Supréme | Chicken breast or game bird |
| Tomates | Tomatoes |
| Terrine | Coarse paté |

**Some dishes you might see on a menu:**

Waterzoi
A variety of
fish in a lush creamy sauce

Soupe de poissons
Fish soup

Rognon de veau rôti
Roasted veal kidney

Ris de veau pêle
Fried veal sweetbread

Faux filet de boeuf
Sirloin steak

Filet de haren mariné
Marinated herring

Carré
d'agneau
Loin of
lamb

149

# Eating Out

Everything has its time and place and that includes lunchtime. In France restaurants are generally open for lunch only between 12noon - 3pm.

If you are in need of sustenance outside these hours look for those restaurants that advertise that they are a "non-stop" restaurant. Otherwise you have no choice but to wait until the evening when the restaurants open again at around 7pm.

Alternative eateries to consider are the crêperies which tend to stay open all day; or even though it seems incongruous with French cuisine, in desparation you could head for a McDonald's for immediate relief.

## Dunkerque

**Bistrot de la Plage**
24 Digue de Mer
Dunkerque Malo Les Bains
Tel: 00 33 (0)328 65 01 11
Tariff: from £9
Open: 11.30-14-30 and 18.30-22.00. Primarily a seafood restaurant also serving regional specialities and salads. The restaurant has a sea view.
**Special offer:** Show your guide and receive either a comlimentary calvados, a Genvière or a coffee.

**Le Grand Morien**
Place Jean Bart
Dunkerque
Tel: 00 33 (0) 328 665518
Tariff: from £7
Open: 19.00-midnight
Brasserie style restaurant
**Special offer:** Show your guide and receive a kir royal and a small plate of cheese.

# Eating Out

## DUNKERQUE contd.

### McArthur
3 rue Belle Vue
Dunkerque
Tel: 00 33 (0)3 28 63 54 63
Tariff: various
Open: Mon-Fri 11.00-02.00
Sat 19.30-02.00.
A pub serving pub grub
French style during
lunchtime. Murphy's and
Heineken are sold. This
pub is regarded as one of
Dunkirk's hot spot.

### Le Roie de la Moule
129 Digue de Mer
Dunkerque Malo les Bains
Tel: 00 33 (0)3 28 69 25 37
'King of the Mussels'
describes the menu well.
There are 9 preparations of
mussel dishes alongside
other seafood.
Tariff: Av. £10
Open: 19.00-midnight
**Special offer:** Show your
guide for a complUementary
"Merry Coffee" - a coffee
with whisky and cream to
round off the meal.

### Les Trois Brasseurs
ZAC Des Bassins
Pôle Marine
Dunkerque
Tel: 00 33 (0)3 28 59 60 60
A restaurant with its own
brewery serving typically
Flemish cooking. The
restaurant is decked out in
brewery style.
**Special offer:** Show your
guide and get a free glass
of beer with your meal.

### Just fifteen minutes from Dunkerque

### Taverne Le Bruegel
1 rue du Marché aux
Fromages
Bergues
Tel: 00 33 (0)3 28 68 19 19
A well presented
restaurant serving Flemish
cuisine such as waterzoi
and andouillette.
**Special offer:** Show your
guide for a free coffee for
every diner in your group.

## Calais

### Aquar'aile
255 rue Jean Moulin
Plage de Calais
Tel: 00 33 (0)321 34 00 00
www.aquaraile.com
On the 4th floor of a block
of seafront flats.
Fine seafood restaurant
Tariff: £15-£45
**Special offer**: On
presentation of your
guide, a brandy or a tipple
to round off the meal.

### La Bigoudène Crêperie
22 rue de la Paix
Calais
Crêpes
Tariff: From £6
**Special offer**: Present
your guide, and receive a
glass of their in-house
drink Kir Breton
(champagne and cider)

### Les Dunes
48 Route National
Blériot Plage, Calais
Tel: 00 33 (0)3 21 34 54 30
Exit 14 off A16 motorway
Seafood restaurant wth a
fine wine list
Tariff: From £10

### Au Cote d'Argent
1 Digue Gaston Berthe
Calais
Tel: 00 33 (0)3 2134 68 07
On the sea front
Quality fish restaurant
Tariff: From £10

### Le Détroit
5 Boulevard de la
Résistance, Calais
Fish, seafood and
woodfire grills
Tariff: From £10

### Restaurant La Mer
30 rue de la Mer
Calais
Tel: 00 33 (0)3 21 96 17 72
A seafood restaurant
open 12 noon to 12
midnight. The menu
includes mussels, grilled
fish and meat dishes.
Tariff: from £6
**Special offer**: 5%
discount on presentation
of your guide

### Le Saint-Charles
47 Place d'Armes
(north side) Calais
Fish - monkfish in cider,
scallops - sirloin steak
Tariff: £7-£20

**Le Channel**
3 Boulevard de la
Résistance, Calais
Tel: 00 33 (0)3 21 34 42 30
A gastronomic restaurant
offering a view of the port
and highly
recommended cuisine
e.g. sweetbreads and
fish.
Tariff: various fixed
priced menus
Tariff: From £10

**Le Milano**
14 Place d'Armes
Calais
Pizzeria
Tariff: £8
**Special Offer**: Present
this guide for a free glass
of wine with your meal.

**Le Sole Meunière**
1 Boulevard de la
Resistance, Calais
Tel: 00 33 (0)3 21 34 43 01
Seafood and steak grills
Tariff: From £10

**Le Grand Bleu**
8 rue Jean-Pierre Avron
Bassin de la Colonne
(opp. Calais port), Calais
Tel: 00 33 (0)3 21 97 97 98
Fish, seafood
Tariff: £10

**Au Calice**
55 Boulevard Jacquard
Calais
Tel: 00 33 (0)3 21 34 51 78
Lovely brasserie café
Tariff: From £5

## Along the D940

**Le Thomé de Gamond**
Mont Hubert
Escalles
Tel: 00 33 (0)3 21 82 32 03
Tariff: From £10
Perched on a mountain top, this seafood restaurant offers a most agreeable environment to spend an afternoon. Each table has a window with a view over the countryside and the food is delicious.
**Special offer:** A bottle of wine to take home when you present this guide.

**Restaurant du Cap**
Place de la Mairie
Escalles
Cap Blanc-Nez
Seafood restaurant
Tariff: From £9

**L'Epicure**
1 rue Gare
Wimereux
Tel: 00 33 (0)3 21 83 21 83
Seafood restaurant
Tariff: £13

**Hôtel de la Plage**
Bar and restaurant
21 rue Gustave Danquin
62164 Audresselles
off the D940
Seafood
Tariff: from £9.50

**Les Dunes**
48 Route National
Bleriot-Plage
Tel: 00 33 (0) 321 34 54 30
Tariff: £10.00 approx

**Le Relais de la Brocante**
2 rue de Ledinghem
Wimille
Tel: 00 33 (0)3 21 83 19 31
Situated in the village close to the church.
The menu includes kipper toast flavoured with coffee beans & tripe sausage with juniper.
Tariff: From £8

**L'Estival**
62179 Audinghen
off the D940 coastal road
Seafood restaurant
Tariff: From £5
**Special offer:** A glass of kir to enjoy with your meal.

# Le Thomé De Gammond

## Have lunch and dinner** on a mountain top

Enjoy wonderful French cuisine with exceptional panoramic views including the Kent coast on a clear day.

**A friendly welcome from the FRECHOU family**

English Channel — Tunnel — CALAIS
Cap Blanc Nez
Escalles — Frethun Terminal
Wissant
Cap Gris Nez — Audinghen — Cap Blanc Exit
Ambleteuse
Wimereux — Marquise
BOULOGNE
D940 / A16

A **FREE** bottle of good wine to take home on production of this advertisement (1 bottle per table)*.

*No further discount applies

### How To Get There
Take the D940 from the Blériot-Plage in Calais centre following the sign 'Boulogne par la corniche'. Follow the D940 road for around 15 minutes. It is situated on the left. From the A16 motorway exit at junction (sortie) 12.

** Saturday evening open 6pm-8.30pm

Groups Welcome

Vegetarian Menu
£9.80

Kids Menu
£4.90

### OTHER MENUS
£9.80, £13.00, £15.00

**Two gastronomic menus:**
£17.00 and £20.05

**Seafood menus:**
£13.80, £16.00 and £16.50

Open 7 days a week from 12 noon to 3.30pm
** July & August - Open in the evening

### LE THOMÉ DE GAMOND RESTAURANT
Situated opposite Cap Blanc Nez on top of Mont d'Hubert above Escalles, France
**Less than10 minutes from Eurotunnel terminal**
Tel: 00 33 (0)3 21 82 32 03
Fax: 00 33 (0)3 21 82 32 61
www.capblancnez.com

## Boulogne

**Le Pot d'Etain**
24 rue du Pot d'Etain
Boulogne
French cuisine
Tariff: From £5

**Le Doyen**
1 rue do Doyen
Boulogne
Tel: 00 33 (0)3 21 30 13 08
French cuisine with
emphasis on fish dishes,
candle-lit.
Tariff: From £9

**Chez Jules**
8 Place Dalton
Boulogne
Tel: 00 33 (0)3 21 31 54 12
A brasserie and a
restaurant so dine or
snack as you please.
Tariff: From £10

**Cave du Fromager**
23 and 30 rue de Lille
Boulogne
Tel: 00 33 (0)3 21 80 49 69
Situated in the old town.
Its casual surroundings
offer an imaginative menu
of cheese dishes.
Tariff: Average £7

**Christophe et Laurence**
10 rue Coquelin
Boulogne
Deli, steak, brasserie.
Tariff: £7.50

**Irish Pub**
6-10 rue Doyen
62200 Boulogne
Off Place Dalton

**Estaminet du Château**
2 rue du Château
Boulogne
French traditional cuisine.
Tariff: £8.50

**Gourmandière**
6 rue des Religieuses
(off rue Faidherbe).
Boulogne
Salads, omelettes,
quiches, traditional food.
Tariff: From £7

**Le Matelote**
80 Boulevard Ste-Beuve
Boulogne
Tel: 00 33 (0)3 21 30 17 97
Situated opposite the
casino. A gastronomic
restaurant specialising in
seafood. Good wine list.
Tariff: £15-£35

**HOTEL-RESTAURANT**

*HAMIOT*

**1-3 rue Faidherbe**
**62200 Boulogne-Sur-Mer**
**Tel: 00 33 (0)321 31 44 20**

*Enjoy varied regional cuisine in warm and stylish surroundings.*

*All our sumptuous dishes are lovingly prepared in true traditional style.*

**Hamiot Hotel Restaurant**
1-3 rue Faidherbe.
Boulogne
Tel: 00 33 (0)3 21 32 44 20
Varied regional cuisine served in nice surroundings.
Tariff: £10

**La Houblonnière**
8 rue Monsigny
Boulogne
Tel: 00 33 (0)3 21 30 55 30
An informal brasserie style restaurant with more than 100 beers including Yorkshire Ruddles.
Tariff: From £7

**L'Huitrière**
11 Place Lorraine
Boulogne
Tel: 00 33 (0)3 21 31 35 27
On pedestrian square. Tiny fish restaurant and oyster bar.
Tariff: £8 and £12

**Restaurant de la Pierre Chaude**
19 rue de Lille
Boulogne
Generally French. Guests cook their own meats on hot grills
Tariff: £7.50-12

**Sucré-Salé**
13 rue Monsigny
off rue Thiers
Boulogne
Tel: 00 33 (0)3 21 33 81 82
This salon de thé which serves pastries and ice cream serves, salads and other savoury dishes.
Tariff: Various

# Eating Out

## Le Touquet

**Flavio**
1 Ave de Verger
Le Touquet
Tel: 00 33 (0)3 21 05 10 22
Flavio offers gastronomic
and highly delicious
cuisine in gorgeous,
elegant surroundings.
Tariff: £23

**Le Café des Arts**
80 rue de Paris,
Le Touquet
Tel: 00 33 (0)3 21 05 21 55
The restaurant offers fine
nouvelle cuisine. The walls
are covered in works of art
which are for sale.
Tariff: £30

**L'Escale**
Aérodrome, Le Touquet
Tel: 00 33 (0)3 21 05 23 22
The large local clientele
confirms the restaurant's
quality cuisine.
Tariff: From £8

**Le Nemo**
Boulevard de la Mer
Le Touquet
Tel: 00 33 (0)3 21 06 20 66
Informal cuisine
Tariff: from £6
Submarine themed decor

**Red Rock Café**
69 rue de Paris
Le Touquet
open to 4am
**Special offer**: 10% off
beers, Barcardi cocktails,
and whisky on
presentation of the guide.

**Les Sports**
22 ru St Jean
Le Touquet
Tel: 00 33 (0)3 21 05 05 22
Tariff: £12
Open all day serving
steaks, and welch rarebit.
Regarded highly locally

## Montreuil-Sur-Mer

**L'Auberge de la Grenouillère**
Rue St Pierre
Montreuil-Sur-Mer
Tel: 00 33 (0)3 21 06 07 22
Nouvelle cuisine
Tariff: £16-£40
This restaurant could have
come straight out of The
Wind in the Willows, with
stone floors and an
extraordinary fresco of La
Fontaine's fable, the toad
and bull.

# FLAVIO★★★★

## LE CLUB DE LA FORÊT

1 Avenue du Verger
Le Touquet
Tel: 00 33 (0)3 21 05 10 22
Fax: 00 33 (0)3 21 05 91 55

www.flavio.fr

*D*ine in exquisite decor and enjoy sumptuous cuisine. The menu changes weekly revealing our chef's culinary genius in creating original cuisine of inspired refinement. Guy, the chef, officiates in the kitchen with his 30 years experience working magic with fish, crustaceans, poultry, vegetables from his garden. The brill in rhubarb wine, the large langoustines baked with spices, the soup of summer and winter truffles, the duck foie gras from the pays de l'Artois all enhanced by the majestic wine cellar. A true feast for the taste buds, to be missed on no account.

Menus from £13.00.
Book your table online.
Closed on Monday except
July & August

### Check Out the Automatic Check-Inns

If you are looking to stay overnight or longer on a budget then any of France's budget hotels may be a good option. For these hotels, functionality is the primary concern, so no room service, luxurious towels, beautiful furniture or scenic views. But they are usually situated close to the motorway networks, so you can check in and out and be back on route with ease.

These hotels operate on an unmanned auto-check-in basis. Entrance is by credit card through a "hole in the wall" using the language of your choice, and offer 24-hour access. The rooms are clean, functional and usually comprise a double and a single bed (bunk) plus a colour TV.

The Formule 1 hotel is cheap at around £19 per night for up to three people but the shower and toilet is communal - most annoying if you get into the shower only to find you have forgotten the soap!

Restaurants are never part of the internal landscape of a budget hotel, but there is a snack vending machine which is always accessible. In the morning a simple continental breakfast, though not cordon bleu, is good value for money at around £2.50 per person.

The majority of hotels in France are one and two

| BUDGET HOTELS IN FRANCE | | | |
|---|---|---|---|
| Name | Room price from FF | Beds/ room | Central Reservation |
| B&B | 160 | 4 | 00 33 2 98 33 75 00 |
| Bonsai | 149 | 3 | 00 33 1 42 46 15 45 |
| Formule 1 | 119 | 3 | 00 33 8 36 68 56 85 |
| Mister Bed | 149 | 4 | 00 33 1 46 14 38 00 |

star hotels and prices tend to vary depending on location and comfort. The chain hotels can generally be relied upon to deliver a good quality of service within their star rating. For instance, you can expect a TV, telephone and an en-suite shower room as part of the package in a two star hotel. A bathroom would cost more.

Chambres d'hôtes are becoming popular in France. These are French style bed and breakfasts, mostly run by ordinary people who have turned their private homes into tourist accommodation. They tend to be cheaper than hotels and give a flavour of French life and character. Breakfast tends to be just a coffee, bread or croissant and maybe cheese. These days, many B&B signs offer an English breakfast and this is testament to the increasing number of British visitors.

A gîte - lodging - situated in the countryside gives a feeling of rural living. The kind of accommodation ranges from a simple room or perhaps an entire house. Contact Gîtes de France for more information on 00 33 1 47 42 20 20.

Châteaux also make for beautiful retreats and are often old castles or country mansions found mainly in rural areas.

## 1 & 2 STAR HOTEL CHAINS IN FRANCE
Tariffs vary between £20-£60 per room

| Name | Central Reservation |
| --- | --- |
| Balladins * | 00 33 1 64 46 49 00 |
| Campanile - Motel style | 00 33 1 64 62 46 46 |
| Ibis-Arcade ** | 00 33 1 69 91 05 63 |
| Logis de France * / ** / *** | 00 33 1 45 84 83 84 |

# Hotels

## Dunkerque

**Borel\*\*\***
6 rue l'Hermite
Dunkerque
Tel: 00 33 (0)3 28 66 29 07
www.hotelhirondelle.com
Tariff: From £38

**Hotel Welcome\*\*\***
37 rue Poincaré
Dunkerque
Tel: 00 33 (0)3 28 59 20 70
Tariff: From £37

**Europ Hotel\*\*\***
13 rue du Leughenaer
Dunkerque
Tel: 00 33 (0)3 28 66 29 07
Tariff: From £37

**L'Hirondelle\*\***
46/48 Avenue Faidherbe
Dunkerque
Tel: 00 33 (0)3 28 63 17 65
www.hotelhirondelle.com
Tariff: From £29
In-house restaurant with fish
specialities.
**Special Offer:** When dining
in the restaurant hotel
guests will receive a free
aperitif.

## Calais

**Formule 1 Hotel**
Ave Charles de Gaulle
62231 Coquelles, Calais
Tel: 00 33 (0)3 21 82 67 00
A budget hotel offering
value for money and easy
access to the motorway.
Tariff: £20.00 approx for
three people

**Bellevue\*\***
Place d'Armes
Calais
Tel: 00 33 (0)3 21 34 53 75
Located in Calais centre,
close to the beach
Tariff: From £20.00

**Metropole\*\*\***
45 Quai du Rhin
Calais
Tel: 00 33 (0)3 21 97 54 00
www.metropolhotel.com
Tariff: £32-£40
A pleasant hotel with its
own secure car park and
mini pub. The hotel offers
very good value for money.
**Special Offer:** Show your
guide and receive a
discount of 10% on the
cost of your room.

# Hotels

**Meurice\*\*\***
5 rue Edmond Roche
Calais
Tel: 00 33 (0)3 21 34 57 03
www.hotel-meurice.fr
Tarrif: £34-£50
Located behind the fine arts
museum and park
Richelieu, this hotel is
undoubtedly **the best three
star hotel in Calais**. Its
decor is very grand and
elegant adorned with
antiques and fine furniture.
The rooms are spacious
and offer a variety of
modern conveniences. It
even has its own
gastronomic restaurant and
secure car park.

**Copthorne\*\*\***
Ave Charles de Gaulle
62231 Coquelles, Calais
Tel: 00 33 (0)3 21 46 60 60
A modern hotel conveniently
located close to the
Eurotunnel terminal and
Cité Europe. It has its own
swimming pool and gym
and seems a favourite
among the business
community.
Tariff:£58-£68

**George V \*\*\***
36 rue Royale
Calais
Tel: 00 33 (0)3 21 97 68 00
Centrally located hotel.
Tariff: £35-£50

**Holiday Inn Garden
Court\*\*\***
Boulevard des Alliés
62100 Calais
Tel: 00 33 (0)3 21 34 69 69
A modern, comfortable hotel.
Tariff: £55-£65

# Hotels

## Boulogne

**Formule 1**
Z.I. de l'inquetrie
Rue Pierre Martin
St Martin les Boulogne
Tel: 00 33 (0)3 21 31 26 28
Tariff: £20 approx

**Hôtel Faidherbe**
12 rue du Château
Boulogne
Tel: 00 33 (0)3 21 31 60 93
Tariff: £45-£50

**Ibis Centre** \*\*
Boulevard Diderot
62200 Boulogne
Tel: 00 33 (0)3 21 30 12 40
Tariff: From £37.00

**Ibis Vieille Ville** \*\*
rue Porte Neuve, Boulogne
Tel: 00 33 (0) 3 21 31 21 01
Tariff: From £37.00

**Metropole**
51 rue Thiers, Boulogne
Tel: 00 33 (0)3 21 31 54 30
Tariff: £35-£50

**Le Mirador**
2,4 rue de la Lampe
Boulogne
Tel: 00 33 (0)3 21 31 38 08
Tariff: £15-30

## Le Touquet

**Park Plaza Hôtel** \*\*\*\*
4 Boulevard de la Canche
Le Touquet
Tel: 00 33 (0)3 21 06 88 88
www.parkplazaww.com
Tariff: From £49
A beautiful hotel located in
the forest with a fabulous
range of Thalgo beauty and
relaxation treatments
.

**Special Offer** at Park Plaza:
20% discount on
accommodation, food and
beverages and all beauty
treaments for stays from
Sunday to Wednesday
inclusive, all year round;
20% discount also applies
throughout February,
November and December
(except New Year's Day)

**The Westminster** \*\*\*\*
Avenue du Verger
Le Touquet
Tel: 00 33 (0)3 21 05 48 48
www.westminster.fr
Tariff: From £50
A magnificently luxurious
hotel. It has its own hall of
fame full of signed
photographs of the rich and
famous politicians and stars.

# Hotels

**Holiday Inn Resort****
Avenue du Maréchal Foch
Le Touquet
Tel: 00 33 (0)3 21 06 85 85
A modern hote.
Tariff: from £79

**Bristol***
17 rue Jean Monner
Le Touquet
Tel: 00 33 (0)3 21 81 54 68
A reasonable hotel.
Tariff: from £55

**Novotel Thalassa***
Plage
Le Touquet
Tel: 00 33 (0)3 21 81 54 68
This hotel is attached to the
Thalassa centre famous for
various healing and
relaxation treatments. There
is a direct route from the
hotel to the centre.
Tariff: from £54

**Red Fox Hotel****
Corner of  rue Saint Jean
and rue de Metz
Le Touquet
Tel: 00 33 (0)3 21 81 54 68
A comfortable two star.
Tariff: from £30
Children under 12 stay free.

## Montreuil-Sur-Mer

**Chambres d'Hôtes
Danièle et Michel Louchez**
77 rue Pierre Ledent
Montreuil sur Mer
Tel: 00 33 (0)321 81 54 68
A really classy Chambre
d'hôtes. Just three rooms
all ensuite - all lovely.

**Château de Montreuil**
4 Chausée Capucins
Montreuil sur Mer
62170 Pas de Calais
Tel: 00 33 (0)3 21 81 53 04
38km South of Boulogne
Tariff: From £85-£150

**Les Hauts de Montreuil***
19-21-23 rue Pierre Ledent
62170 Montreuil-Sur-Mer
Tel: 00 33 (0)3 21 81 95 92
Tariff: From £50-£100
per person per night.
The hotel is in the oldest
building in Montreuil with
some parts of the building
dating back to 1537.  It has
its own gastronomic
restaurant and a Caribbean
style restaurant.

# How Much Can You Bring Back?

***In theory there are no limits on the amount of alcohol or tobacco for personal use.
In practice exceeding the Advisory Guidelines, means you could be stopped***

Since 1st January 1993, you are permitted to bring back as much alcohol and tobacco as you like, but it must be for personal use only. So you can happily stock up for Christmas or parties or weddings.

Although H. M. Customs and Excise have no authority to limit the amount you bring back into this country they do have the right to stop you if your purchases exceed the Advisory Guidelines. In this case you may be required to prove that the goods are for your own personal use.

If you are stopped, remember that the H.M. Customs officer is looking for bootleggers or those intent on resale and your co-operation will be appreciated. Other products such as mineral water, or any other non-alcoholic or food products, are not limited in any way.

Enjoy.

## Advisory Guidelines
### as set by H.M. Customs & Excise

| | |
|---|---:|
| Wine (not to exceed 60 litres of sparkling wine) | 90 litres |
| Spirits | 10 litres |
| Intermediate products (i.e port & sherry) | 20 litres |
| Beer | 110 litres |
| Cigarettes | 800 |
| Cigars | 200 |
| Cigarillos | 400 |
| Tobacco | 1 kilogram |

Note: People under 17 are not allowed to bring in tobacco and alcohol

# Conversion Tables

## What's Your Size?
### When buying clothes in France, check the conversion tables below to find out your size:

### Women's Shoes

| GB | | FR | GB | | FR |
|---|---|---|---|---|---|
| 3 | = | 35¹/₂ | 5¹/₂ | = | 39 |
| 3¹/₂ | = | 36 | 6 | = | 39¹/₂ |
| 4 | = | 37 | 6¹/₂ | = | 40 |
| 4¹/₂ | = | 37¹/₂ | 7 | = | 40¹/₂ |
| 5 | = | 38 | 8 | = | 41¹/₂ |

### Women's Dresses/Suits

| GB | | FR | GB | | FR |
|---|---|---|---|---|---|
| 8 | = | 36 | 14 | = | 42 |
| 10 | = | 38 | 16 | = | 44 |
| 12 | = | 40 | 18 | = | 46 |

### Women's Blouses/Sweaters

| GB | | FR | GB | | FR |
|---|---|---|---|---|---|
| 30 | = | 36 | 36 | = | 42 |
| 32 | = | 38 | 38 | = | 44 |
| 34 | = | 40 | 40 | = | 46 |

### Men's Shirts

| GB | FR | GB | | FR |
|---|---|---|---|---|
| 14¹/₂= | 37 | 16 | = | 41 |
| 15 = | 38 | 16¹/₂ | = | 42 |
| 15¹/₂= | 39/40 | 17 | = | 43 |

### Men's Suits

| GB | | FR | GB | | FR |
|---|---|---|---|---|---|
| 36 | = | 46 | 42 | = | 52 |
| 38 | = | 48 | 44 | = | 54 |
| 40 | = | 50 | 46 | = | 56 |

### Men's Shoes

| GB | | FR | GB | | FR |
|---|---|---|---|---|---|
| 7 | = | 40 | 10 | = | 43 |
| 8 | = | 41 | 11 | = | 44 |
| 9 | = | 42 | 12 | = | 45 |
| | | | 13 | = | 46 |

### Weights and Measures:

| | | |
|---|---|---|
| Distance 1.6 km= | | 1 mile |
| Weight 1 kg | = | 2.20lbs |
| Liquid 4.54 litres= | | 1 gallon |
| Liquid 1 litre | = | 1.76 pints |
| Length 1m | = | 39.37inches |
| Area 1sq metre | = | 1.196 sq yds |

### Speed

| kpm | mph | kpm | mph |
|---|---|---|---|
| 50 | 31 | 100 | 62 |
| 70 | 43 | 110 | 68 |
| 80 | 50 | 120 | 75 |
| 90 | 56 | 130 | 81 |

# Out and About in France

*A few essential tips*
*to make your*
*travels a little easier ...*

## En Route:
To comply with French motoring regulations, please note what is and is not essential:

## It is essential:
- To have a full UK driving licence and all motoring documents.
- To be over the age of 18 - even if you have passed your test in the UK.
- Not to exceed 90km/h in the first year after passing your test.
- To display a GB sticker or Euro number plate.
- To carry a red warning triangle.
- To wear rear seat belts if fitted.
- To affix headlamp diverters. These are widely available in motoring shops or DIY with black masking tape.

## It is not essential:
- To have a green card
- To have yellow headlights.

## Parking:
Illegal parking in France can be penalised by a fine, wheel clamping or vehicle removal. Park wherever you see a white dotted line or if there are no markings at all.

There are also numerous pay and display meters. (horodateurs) where small change is required to buy a ticket. The ticket should be displayed inside the car windscreen on the driver's side.

If you find a blue parking zone (zone bleue), this will be indicated by a blue line on the pavement or road and a blue signpost with a white letter P. If there is a square under the P then you have to display a cardboard disc which has various times on it. They allow up to two and a half hours parking time. The discs are available in supermarkets or petrol stations and are sometimes given away free. Ask for a **disque de stationnement.**

## Motorways & Roads:

French motorways (autoroutes) are marked by blue and white A signs. Many motorways are privately owned and outside towns a toll charge (péage) is usually payable and can be expensive. This can be paid by credit card (Visa Card, Eurocard, Mastercard), cash or even coins at automatic gates, so be prepared. Contact a tourist board for the exact cost. if you have access to the internet click on **www.autoroutes.fr.**

Roads are indicated as:

A roads -
Autoroutes - Motorways

D roads -
Routes départementales - scenic alternatives to A roads.

C roads -
routes communales - country roads.

'N Roads -
routes nationales - toll free, single lane roads. Slower than A roads.

## Breakdown on Motorways:

If you should break down on the motorway and you do not have breakdown cover, **DON'T PANIC** you can still get assistance. There are emergency telephones stationed every mile and a half on the motorway. These are directly linked to the local police station. The police are able to locate you automatically and arrange for an approved repair service to come to your aid.

Naturally there is a cost for

---

**IMPORTANT!**

IF THERE ARE NO STOP SIGNS AT INTERSECTIONS, CARS MUST YIELD TO THE RIGHT

---

# joy peace of mind cover at home and abroad

## with Green Flag European Services

you know that **Green Flag** offers
xtensive range of European Services
ring you peace of mind throughout
visit to Europe?

vell as offering an exceptional UK
cle rescue service to its 4 million
nbers, **Green Flag** offers a
prehensive range of motoring
travel-related European Services
oth members and non-members.

following services are available
on-members:

### pean Motoring Assistance

European Motoring Assistance
kage brings you complete peace
ind in the event of a breakdown,
dent, fire or theft whilst abroad.
cludes passenger and vehicle
atriation if needed.

### pean Travel Insurance

policy brings you cover for a
ty of situations including injury,
ellation of your holiday, theft of

your property, additional accommodation
costs and legal expenses.

### Ferry and Eurotunnel Booking Service

**Green Flag** can help you with your
travel plans by booking your channel
crossing at a time which fits in with your
travel plans. We also offer valuable
discounts on selected ferry crossings and
our experienced operators can offer
helpful advice.

All **Green Flag** European Services offer
high standards at great value for money
prices. So next time you're planning a
visit to Europe, give us a call.

### Call European Services FREE
# 0800 400 638

**Green Flag**
Motoring Assistance

this and fees are regulated. Expect to pay around £50 for labour plus parts and around £55 for towing.

An extra 25% supplement is also charged if you break down between 6pm and 8am and any time on Saturdays, Sundays and national holidays.

At the garage, ensure you ask for un Ordre de Réparation (repair quote) which you should sign. This specifies the exact nature of the repairs, how long it will take to repair your vehicle and, most importantly, the cost!

## Traffic News:
Tune in to Autoroute FM107.7 for French traffic news in English and French.

---

**IMPORTANT!**
CHILDREN UNDER 10 ARE NOT ALLOWED TO TRAVEL IN THE FRONT

---

**IMPORTANT!**
DRIVE ON THE RIGHT, OVERTAKE ON THE LEFT

---

**Emergency Phrases:**

Please, help
*Aidez-moi s'il vous plaît*

My car has broken down
*Ma voiture est en panne*

I have run out of petrol
*Je suis en panne d'essence*

The engine is overheating
*Le moteur surchauffe*

There is a problem with the brakes
*Il y a un problème de freins*

I have a flat tyre
*J'ai un pneu crevé*

The battery is flat
*La batterie est vide*

There is a leak in the petrol tank/in the radiator
*Il y a une fuite dans le réservoir d'essence/dans le radiateur*

Can you send a mechanic/breakdown van?
*Pouvez-vous envoyer un mécanicien/une dépanneuse?*

Can you tow me to a garage?
*Pouvez-vous me remorquer jusqu'à un garage?*

I have had an accident
*J'ai eu un accident*

The windscreen is shattered
*Le pare-brise est cassé*

Call an ambulance
*Appelez une ambulance*

# Out and About in France

## Speed Limits:
In France speed limits are shown in kilometres per hour not miles per hour. Always adhere to these speed limits as in France they are strictly enforced:

|  | MPH | km/h |
|---|---|---|
| Toll motorways | 81 | 130 |
| Dual Carriageways | 69 | 110 |
| Other Roads | 55 | 90 |
| Towns | 31 | 50 |

When raining, these speed limits are reduced by 6mph on the roads and 12mph on the motorway. In fog, speed is restricted to 31mph. As well as speed traps, it is useful to know that entrance and exit times through the toll booths can be checked on your toll ticket and may be used as evidence of speeding!

## Roadside Messages:
For safety's sake, it is very important to be aware of the roadside messages:

| | |
|---|---|
| Carrefour | Crossroad |
| Déviation | Diversion |
| Priorité à droite | |
| Give way to traffic on the right | |
| Péage | Toll |
| Ralentir | Slow down |

| | |
|---|---|
| Vous n'avez pas la priorité | |
| | Give way |
| Rappel | Restriction continues |
| Sens unique | One way |
| Serrez à droite/ | Keep right/ |
| à gauche | Keep left |
| Véhicules lents | |
| | Slow vehicles |
| Gravillons | Loose chippings |
| Chaussée Déformée | |
| Uneven road and temporary | |
| | surface |
| Nids de Poules | Potholes |

## Tyre Pressure:
It is crucial to ensure that your tyres are at the correct pressure to cater for heavy loads. Make sure you do not exceed the car's maximum carrying weight. The following table gives a guide to typical loads:

| | | Weight | |
|---|---|---|---|
| 1 case of | Qty | kg | lbs |
| Wine | x 2 | 15kg | 33lbs |
| Champagne | x12 | 22kg | 48lbs |
| Beer 25cl | x 2 | 8kg | 18lbs |

## Drink Driving:
UK drink/drive laws are mild at 80mg alcohol, compared to France. French law dictates that a 50g limit of alcohol is allowed - just one glass of wine. Exceeding

# Out and About in France

this limit risks confiscation of your licence, impounding of the car, a prison sentence or an on-the-spot fine between £20 to £3,000!

## Filling Up:

To fill up, head for petrol stations attached to the hypermarkets as these offer the best value fuel. Petrol stations on the motorway - autoroutes - tend to be the most expensive. Though sterling and travellers cheques are not accepted, credit cards usually are. Some petrol stations have automated payment facilities by credit card. These are generally 24 hour petrol stations and tend to be unmanned in the evening but do not rely on them for fuel salvation as they often do not accept international credit cards!

Currently petrol and diesel are cheaper in France.

Petrol grades are as follows:

## Unleaded petrol -

l'essence sans plomb. Available in 95 & 98 grades - equates to UK premium and super grades respectively.

## Leaded petrol -

l'essence or Super Graded as: 90 octane (2 star), 93 octane (3 star) 97 octane (4 star). Gazole - Diesel Fuel GPL - LPG (liquefied petroleum gas)

## Caught on the Hop!

Cafés allow you to use their toilets for free. Shopping centres also have facilities. If you see a white saucer, place a coin or two in it. In the streets you may come across the Sanisette, a white cylindrical building. Insert the required coin in the slot to open the door. After use the Sanisette scrubs itself.

## Shopping

To use your credit card ensure that you have your passport handy as you may be expected to produce it. Shops and supermarkets open and close as follows:

Open                     9.00 am
Close lunch-time 12.00 noon
Open again          2.00 pm
Close finally  5.00-7.00 pm
Most shops are closed on Sunday and some on Monday.

# Out and About in France

## Shopping:
Supermarket trolleys (les chariots) require a (refundable) 10 franc piece.

## Taxi!
It is cheaper to hail a taxi in the street or cab ranks indicated by the letter 'T' than order one by telephone. This is because a telephone-requested taxi will charge for the time taken to reach you. Taxi charges are regulated. The meter must show the minimum rate on departure and the total amount (tax included) on arrival. If the driver agrees that you share the taxi, he has the right to turn the meter back to zero at each stop showing the minimum charge again. A tip *(pourboire)* is expected. It is customary to pay 10-15%.

## No Smoking!
The French have an etiquette for everything and that includes smoking. It is forbidden to smoke in public places. However, there are quite often spaces reserved in cafés and restaurants for smokers.

## Public Holidays:
Most French shops will be shut on the following days

| Jan 1 | New Year | Jour de l'an |
|---|---|---|
| Apr* | Easter Monday | Lundi de Pâques |
| May 1 | Labour Day | Fête du Travail |
| May 8 | Victory Day | Armistice 1945 |
| May* | Ascension | Ascension |
| May* | Whitsun | Lundi de Pentecôte |
| July 14 | Bastille Day | Fête nationale |
| Aug 15 | Assumption | Assomption |
| Nov 1 | All Saints' | Toussaint |
| Nov 11 | Armistice Day | Armistice 1918 |
| Dec 25 | Christmas | Noël |
| *Dates change each year. | | |

## Tipping:
Tipping is widely accepted in France. However, restaurant menus with the words 'servis compris' indicate that service is included but small change can be left if so desired. The following is the accepted norm for tipping:

| Restaurants service usually included | Optional |
|---|---|
| Cafés service usually included | Optional |
| Hotels | No |
| Hairdressers | 10F |
| Taxis | 10F |
| Porters | 10F |
| Cloakroom attendants | Small change |
| Toilets | Small change |

# Out and About in France

## Phoning Home:
Phonecards (Télécartes) are widely used and available at travel centres, post offices, tobacconists and shops displaying the Télécarte sign.

Cheap rate (50% extra time) is between 22.30hrs-08.00hrs Monday to Friday, 14.00hrs-08.00hrs Saturday, all day Sunday & public holidays.

To call the UK dial 00, at the dialling tone dial 44 followed by the phone number and omit 0 from the STD code.

## Writing Home:
Post offices (PTT) are open Monday to Friday during office hours and half day on Saturday. Smaller branches tend to close between noon and 2pm.

Stamps can also be purchased from tobacconists.

The small but bright yellow post boxes are easy to spot

## Money Matters:

### Currency:
French currency, known as the French Franc is shown in 3 ways: FF, Fr or F. A Franc is roughly equivalent to 11p.

The French Franc is made up of 100 centimes.

Centimes have their own set of coins *(pièces)* i.e. 5, 10, 20 and 50 centimes - marked as 1/2F.

Francs are in 1, 2, 5, 10 and 20F pieces and bank notes *(billets)* are in 20, 50, 100, 200 and 500F notes.

When you are looking at a price tag, menu or receive a receipt be aware that unlike the British system of separating pounds and pence with a decimal point, in France there is no decimal point, the francs and centimes are separated by a comma

Unlimited currency may be taken into France but you must declare bank notes of 50,000 French francs or

# Out and About in France

more if you are bringing this back. **Note:** The euro became legal currency in France on January 1999. All prices are displayed in French francs and euros. The Franc will be phased out on 30th June 2002.

**Currency Exchange:**
Changing money from sterling to French francs can be expensive. Use your credit card to pay for goods abroad, as credit card companies give a better rate of exchange and do not chargecommission when buying goods abroad. Of course you will require some cash. Change your money in the UK where it can be a little more competitive than in France.

In France you can also change money and cash travellers cheques at the post office (PTT), banks, stations and private bureaux de change. Hypermarket complexes have machines available to change your sterling to French francs. AVOID these as they are expensive It would be better

to make a purchase in the hypermarket in sterling, as change is given in French francs without commission. Though convenient, always be aware of the exchange rate. Some shops take advantage.

French franc travellers cheques can be used as cash and if you wish to turn them into cash at a French bank you will receive the face value - no commission. **Most banks in France do not accept Eurocheques**

**Credit Cards:**
If your card has been rejected in a shop or restaurant, it could be that their card reading machine does not recognise it - some French credit cards have a 'puce', a microchip with security information on it. British cards do not In this event, French tourist authorities recommend you say:
*Les cartes anglaises ne sont pas des cartes à puce, mais à band magnétique. Ma carte est valable et je vous serais reconnaissant d'en*

# Out and About in France

*demander la confirmation
auprès de votre banque ou
de votre centre de
traitement.'*

**which means**

*English cards don't have an
information chip, but a
magnetic band. My card is
valid and I would be grateful
if you would confirm this
with your bank or
processing centre.'*

If you need to contact
**Barclaycard**
Tel: +44 (0)1604 234234
**Visa**
Tel: +44 (0)1383 621166
**Visa in France**
Tel: 01 45 67 84 84

## Cashpoints

You can use your cashpoint
card to get local currency
fromcash-dispensing
machines. This service is
available at major banks
such as: Crédit Lyonnais,
Crédit Agricole and Crédit
Mutuel. If the machine bears
the same logo as that
displayed on your card,
such as Visa or Delta, then
you can insert your card and
follow the instructions.
These are likely to be in

English as your card will be
recognised as British.
Punch in your PIN and
press the button marked
**Envoi.** When prompted tell
the machine how much you
want in French francs. You
will see phrases such as:

**Tapez votre code secret**
Enter your pin
**Veuillez patienter -**
Please wait
**Opération en cours -**
Money on its way!

## Pharmacie

These are recognised by
their green cross sign. Staff
tend to be highly qualified
so are able to give medical
advice on minor ailments,
provide first aid and
prescribe a range of drugs
Some drugs are only
available via a doctor's
prescription (ordonnance).

## Doctor

Any pharmacie will have an
address of a doctor.
Consultation fees are
generally about £15.00.
Ask for a Feuille de Soins
(Statement of Treatment) if
you are insured.

## Medical Aid

As members of the EU, the British can get urgent medical treatment in France at reduced costs on production of a form E111 available from the Department of Health and Social Security. A refund can then be obtained in person or by post from the local Social Security Offices (Caisse Primaire d'Assurance Maladie).

## Passports:

Before travelling to France you need a full 10- year British passport. Non--British nationals require a visa and regulations vary according to your nationality. Contact the French Consulate.

## Pet Passports:

Since 28th February 2000, a scheme has been in force enabling cats and dogs to travel abroad without being subjected to six months quarantine. A blood test is required and a microchip fitted. Not more than 48 hours before return the animal must be treated for ticks and tapeworms. Only

then will it be awarded the official pet passport'. Further information is available from PETS helpline 08702411710.

## What's the Time?

French summer starts on the last Sunday in March at 2am and ends on the last Sunday in October at 3am. Time is based on Central European Time (Greenwich Mean Time + 1 hour in winter and + 2 hours in summer). France is one hour ahead. The clocks are put forward 1 hour in the spring and put back 1 hour in the autumn.

## Electricity:

You will need a continental adapter plug (with round pins). The voltage in France is 220V and 240V in the UK.

## Television/Video Tapes

French standard TV broadcast system is SECAM whereas in the UK it is PAL. Ordinary video cassettes bought in France will show only in black and white. French video tapes cannot be played on British videos. Ask for VHS PAL system.

# Quick Currency Converter

| £ | FF@ 9.50 | €@ 1.60 | £ | FF@ 9.50 | €@ 1.60 | £ | £@ 9.50 | €@ 1.60 |
|---|---|---|---|---|---|---|---|---|
| 1 | 9.50 | 1.60 | 49 | 465.50 | 78.40 | 97 | 921.50 | 155.20 |
| 2 | 19.00 | 3.20 | 50 | 475.00 | 80.00 | 98 | 931.00 | 156.80 |
| 3 | 28.00 | 4.80 | 51 | 484.50 | 81.60 | 99 | 940.50 | 158.40 |
| 4 | 38.00 | 6.40 | 52 | 494.00 | 83.20 | 100 | 950.00 | 160.00 |
| 5 | 47.50 | 8.00 | 53 | 503.50 | 84.80 | 101 | 959.50 | 161.60 |
| 6 | 57.00 | 9.60 | 54 | 513.00 | 86.40 | 102 | 969.00 | 163.20 |
| 7 | 66.50 | 11.20 | 55 | 522.50 | 88.00 | 103 | 978.50 | 164.80 |
| 8 | 76.00 | 12.80 | 56 | 532.00 | 89.60 | 104 | 988.00 | 166.40 |
| 9 | 85.50 | 14.40 | 57 | 541.50 | 91.20 | 105 | 997.50 | 168.00 |
| 10 | 95.00 | 16.00 | 58 | 551.00 | 92.80 | 106 | 1007.00 | 169.60 |
| 11 | 104.50 | 17.60 | 59 | 560.50 | 94.40 | 107 | 1016.50 | 171.20 |
| 12 | 114.00 | 19.20 | 60 | 570.00 | 96.00 | 108 | 1026.00 | 172.80 |
| 13 | 123.50 | 20.80 | 61 | 579.50 | 97.60 | 109 | 1035.50 | 174.40 |
| 14 | 133.00 | 22.40 | 62 | 589.00 | 99.20 | 110 | 1045.00 | 176.00 |
| 15 | 142.50 | 24.00 | 63 | 598.50 | 100.80 | 111 | 1054.50 | 177.60 |
| 16 | 150.57 | 25.60 | 64 | 608.00 | 102.40 | 112 | 1064.00 | 179.20 |
| 17 | 161.50 | 27.20 | 65 | 617.50 | 104.00 | 113 | 1073.50 | 180.80 |
| 18 | 171.00 | 28.80 | 66 | 627.00 | 105.60 | 114 | 1083.00 | 182.40 |
| 19 | 180.50 | 30.40 | 67 | 636.50 | 107.20 | 115 | 1092.50 | 184.00 |
| 20 | 190.00 | 32.00 | 68 | 646.00 | 108.80 | 116 | 1102.00 | 185.60 |
| 21 | 199.50 | 33.60 | 69 | 655.50 | 110.40 | 117 | 1111.50 | 187.20 |
| 22 | 209.00 | 35.30 | 70 | 665.00 | 112.00 | 118 | 1121.00 | 188.80 |
| 23 | 218.50 | 36.80 | 71 | 674.50 | 113.60 | 119 | 1130.50 | 190.40 |
| 24 | 228.00 | 38.40 | 72 | 684.00 | 115.20 | 120 | 1140.00 | 192.00 |
| 25 | 237.50 | 40.00 | 73 | 693.50 | 116.80 | 121 | 1149.50 | 193.60 |
| 26 | 247.00 | 41.60 | 74 | 703.00 | 118.40 | 122 | 1159.00 | 195.20 |
| 27 | 256.50 | 43.20 | 75 | 712.50 | 120.00 | 123 | 1168.50 | 196.90 |
| 28 | 266.00 | 44.80 | 76 | 722.00 | 121.60 | 124 | 1178.00 | 198.40 |
| 29 | 275.50 | 46.40 | 77 | 731.50 | 123.20 | 125 | 1187.50 | 200.00 |
| 30 | 285.00 | 48.00 | 78 | 741.00 | 124.80 | 126 | 1197.00 | 201.60 |
| 31 | 294.50 | 49.60 | 79 | 750.50 | 126.40 | 127 | 1206.50 | 203.20 |
| 32 | 304.00 | 51.20 | 80 | 760.00 | 128.00 | 128 | 1216.00 | 204.80 |
| 33 | 313.50 | 52.80 | 81 | 769.50 | 129.60 | 129 | 1225.50 | 206.40 |
| 34 | 323.00 | 54.40 | 82 | 779.00 | 131.20 | 130 | 1235.00 | 208.00 |
| 35 | 332.50 | 56.00 | 83 | 788.50 | 132.80 | 131 | 1244.50 | 209.60 |
| 36 | 342.00 | 57.60 | 84 | 798.00 | 134.40 | 132 | 1254.00 | 211.20 |
| 37 | 351.50 | 59.20 | 85 | 805.90 | 136.00 | 133 | 1263.50 | 212.80 |
| 38 | 361.00 | 60.80 | 86 | 815.40 | 137.60 | 134 | 1273.00 | 214.40 |
| 39 | 370.50 | 62.40 | 87 | 824.90 | 139.20 | 135 | 1282.50 | 216.00 |
| 40 | 380.00 | 64.00 | 88 | 834.40 | 140.80 | 136 | 1292.00 | 217.60 |
| 41 | 389.50 | 65.60 | 89 | 843.90 | 142.40 | 137 | 1301.50 | 219.20 |
| 42 | 399.00 | 67.20 | 90 | 853.40 | 144.00 | 138 | 1311.00 | 220.80 |
| 43 | 408.50 | 68.80 | 91 | 862.90 | 145.60 | 139 | 1320.50 | 361.40 |
| 44 | 418.00 | 70.40 | 92 | 872.40 | 147.20 | 140 | 1330.00 | 224.00 |
| 45 | 427.50 | 72.00 | 93 | 883.50 | 148.80 | 145 | 1377.50 | 232.00 |
| 46 | 437.00 | 73.60 | 94 | 893.00 | 150.40 | 150 | 1425.00 | 240.00 |
| 47 | 446.50 | 75.20 | 95 | 902.50 | 152.00 | 175 | 1662.50 | 280.00 |
| 48 | 456.00 | 76.80 | 96 | 912.00 | 153.60 | 200 | 1900.00 | 320.00 |